LET'S GET STARTED

WITH PEPPER BELLY PETE

83
press

LET'S GET STARTED

WITH PEPPER BELLY PETE

N. DEE WILLIAMS

83 press®

Copyright © 2024 by 83 Press

83 Press
2323 2nd Avenue North
Birmingham, AL 35203
83press.com

ISBN: 979-8-9874820-6-3
Printed in China

CONTENTS

I'd like to dedicate this book to my son, Wylie (who also goes by Pepperoni Pete on my videos). He's the whole reason I started doing all of this. I wanted to teach him how to cook at a young age so that he'd be able to take care of himself when he got older. I enjoy spending time with him in the kitchen and making meals for him. I'm thankful for who he is, and I'm proud of the person he's becoming. I hope we get to fry, grill, bake, and roast together for many years to come.

—N. Dee Williams

A HEART
THE SIZE OF TEXAS

Foreword by Jack Wilkerson

N. Dee Williams is a special guy, and I'm lucky enough to be his father-in-law. He's been a wonderful husband to my daughter—they make a great team. He's not a hard guy to say good things about. He has a lot of gifts. Most people would think his greatest gifts are cooking and making videos for social media, but I disagree. His greatest gift is being a wonderful father to my grandson, Wylie.

When he and my daughter, Sara, got married and decided to have a baby, I wasn't sure if he was ready to be a father. N. Dee had no experience with children and had been an only child himself. He started to research everything he could about raising children. By the time Wylie was a year old, N. Dee knew more than I did about raising kids—and I had already raised two to adulthood!

Then, when COVID-19 hit, he really took the bull by the horns. He decided to homeschool Wylie, who was in kindergarten. He consulted some retired teachers he knew and made a plan. He did a fantastic job being Wylie's teacher. He wanted Wylie to enjoy it, so he made it entertaining. He started recording some of their school sessions and putting them on Facebook—he called it N. Dee ISD (Independent School District). He took what could have been a traumatic experience during a global pandemic and turned it into something fun for Wylie. And when Wylie went back to school, he was on grade level and even ahead of where he should have been in some cases.

If there's ever been a gentle giant, it's N. Dee. He can do so many things, and he will truly do anything for anybody. He's a lot of fun to be around and never has a bad day. I admire the way he looks at life. His goal in every undertaking, whether it's fatherhood or fishing, is to do it to the best of his ability. I'm so proud for him about this cookbook. He loves to feed his family, and I know he wants to help other folks do the same.

INTRODUCTION

I grew up in east Texas, which is where I still live now—in the house I grew up in on land my grandparents owned. I was named after my dad, Norman Dee. He was a bulldozer operator for most of his life and then worked for the postal service his last few years. I learned to cook from my family. I'd help my mom with cookies and things from time to time. She cooked every day. Both my parents worked, so my great aunt came and stayed with me every summer and cooked a lot. So really, I just watched my mom and my great aunt as I was growing up and picked up things from them. I knew that I liked to eat, so I figured out how to cook!

My mom liked to cook, but she worked full-time for 40-something years. She'd be too tired to cook by the time she got home after work, but she felt like she needed to make dinner for her family. So, she'd get up at 4:30 in the morning and make a full meal—pork chops, green beans, and mashed potatoes. We'd eat it for breakfast. That was what we did every day during the week. On the weekends, she'd cook at normal times. Man, everything she made was great. My favorites were pinto beans, cornbread, mashed potatoes, and fried hamburgers and gravy. For my birthday, she'd always make me a yellow cake with chocolate icing.

Growing up, I spent a lot of time with extended family. I was an only child, but I had cousins to play with. My cousin Kyle and I would ride go-karts and go fishing together. I got a Ram pickup truck before I turned 16. Kyle and I spent all summer doing circles in the field and listening to music. I was really into speakers and loud music. I even cut a hole in the truck between the cab and the bed for a huge speaker. I was vibrating rooms in homes across the street!

My wife, Sara, and I went to the same high school. I was older than she was, so we didn't meet until later. We got married in 2010 and had our son, Wylie, in 2015. I'd spent most of my adult life working for the state before I ended up at home for a little bit on short-term disability because of bone spurs in my feet that meant I couldn't stand all day long anymore. The year before, I had homeschooled Wylie for kindergarten during the COVID-19 pandemic. I had made some videos of that time to put on Facebook, and my friends and family really enjoyed it. I had seen that there were these

other cooks out there making videos about food. I figured I could do that, too, so I just went in the kitchen and gave it a try. My first videos got several hundred thousand views, and I figured that was pretty good.

I just kept going with them once they took off. The first video that went viral was the Chicken Fried Egg. I made it up that day—I had never even done it before. I just did it, and it worked on the video. It got a million videos in one day. The Pioneer Woman's team contacted me to ask if they could write an article about it to include in her magazine. That was about three weeks after I started making cooking videos from my kitchen. My most-viewed recipe to date is the Modified Mississippi Pot Roast. It went viral on all the platforms and has more than 200 million views.

Zippy-Zap Sauce was my first product. That came out about a year after I started making videos. I can't believe how many people buy the sauce and how far spread the reach is. People from all over (in every state) buy the sauce. I'm excited to see where things go from here. For now, I'm just going to keep making videos and putting them out there. I've got some big partnerships that are starting to happen and think there could be some good things in the works. Having this cookbook and getting a new way to share recipes is something I feel proud about. I hope I've taught people to be willing to try some new things and that cooking can be fun. It doesn't have to be all that serious all the time. Just get in the kitchen and see what you can make. Teach your kids how to cook and pass it down. Have friends over for hamburgers to watch a game. Or try an old family recipe you've never made yourself. Life's about enjoying the good times, and for a lot of folks (the ones I like having around anyway), that means good food! Now, let's get started! ＼

SACUL
TEXAS
POP. 150

IT DOESN'T MATTER IF IT'S A BLACK-TIE EVENT
IN BEVERLY HILLS OR A PASTURE PARTY DOWN
BY THE RIVER BOTTOM, FOLKS JUST WANT TO
EAT FOOD THAT TASTES GOOD.

INVITE 'EM OVER!

THERE'S NOTHING LIKE HAVING your friends and family over to you house to share a meal. Whether you're grilling burgers for the game on TV or sitting down for Thanksgiving dinner, life's always more fun when food and people are involved! We're fortunate to have some good family and friends— heck, most of 'em are also my neighbors. I think I'm kin to just about everybody who lives on my road. The point is, if you're lucky enough to have good folks in your life, make sure you spend time with them. Last summer, I cooked up some ribs and a few other things and told everybody to come on by. These are some pictures from that day. We all just hung out in the yard and had a good ole time. Things don't have to be fancy to be good. Enjoy what you have with the people who matter to you.

A LOT OF PEOPLE ASK, "WHERE'D YA GET THE NAME 'PEPPER BELLY PETE'?"

I had an uncle named Pete who was always really entertaining. I wanted a name that meant something to me and could be relatable to my audience. I eat a lot of spicy foods and use peppers we love here in Texas. In fact, when I make food for my videos, I have to turn down the heat. If I make it for myself, no one else will be able to eat it! I used to have a habanero plant. I'd pull the peppers off and eat them fresh. So, peppers and Pete . . . It just made sense to me.

Some people think I talk funny, but it's not that hard to understand. Here's a little key to figuring out a few of my favorite sayings:

TEXAS TRINITY = onion, garlic, and jalapeño pepper
WORSHYOURSISTER SAUCE = Worcestershire Sauce
JARLIC = jarred garlic
AIRLESS FRYER = deep fryer

Y'all have been asking for a cookbook for a long time, but sometimes it's helpful to see the recipe in action. I've put QR codes in the book for some of my favorite recipes in case you want to see how it all comes together. I don't make my recipes the exact same way every time, so if in doubt, follow the typed recipe. You can make changes to these recipes based on what your family likes best. It's all about getting in the kitchen and making something good!

CHAPTER 1

BOLD

BREAKFASTS

GET YOUR DAY STARTED OFF RIGHT
WITH A HEARTY BREAKFAST AND FULL
STOMACH. THEN GO UNHITCH YOUR
HORSE AND GET ON TO WORK.

Breakfast Taco

Makes 2 servings

You've probably heard of breakfast tacos, but have you ever seen one with a shell made just from cheese? Now you have!

1 cup shredded Cheddar-Jack cheese blend, divided
4 slices bacon
2 large eggs, divided
½ teaspoon kosher salt, divided
½ teaspoon ground black pepper, divided
1 avocado (peeled, pitted, and chopped), divided
Topping: pico de gallo

1. In a medium nonstick skillet, cook ½ cup cheese over medium heat until melted and bubbly. Remove from skillet, and place on a parchment-lined pan. Repeat with remaining ½ cup cheese.
2. In a medium cast-iron skillet, cook bacon over medium heat until crispy, 2 to 3 minutes. Remove, reserving drippings in the skillet, and let drain on paper towels. Add 1 egg, ¼ teaspoon salt, and ¼ teaspoon pepper; cook until egg white is set, 3 to 4 minutes. Carefully flip egg, and cook for 30 seconds more. Remove from skillet, and repeat with remaining egg, remaining ¼ teaspoon salt, and remaining ¼ teaspoon pepper.
3. Place cheese on plate; top with 1 egg, 2 slices bacon, and half of avocado. Repeat with remaining cheese, remaining egg, remaining bacon, and remaining avocado. Top with pico de gallo, if desired. Fold cheese like a tortilla shell, and eat like a taco.

Ranch Hand Breakfast Casserole

Makes about 8 servings

Whether you're getting ready for a hard day's work out on the ranch or you're heading into the office, this casserole is sure to set you up right.

1 (32-ounce) bag frozen Tater Tots
1 (12-ounce) package bacon, chopped
1 pound ground breakfast sausage
1 small red onion, diced
1 (4-ounce) can hot diced green chiles
1 tablespoon plus ¼ teaspoon ground black pepper, divided
1 teaspoon garlic powder
⅓ cup all-purpose flour
2 cups plus 2 tablespoons half-and-half (or whole milk), divided
3 cups shredded Colby-Jack cheese blend, divided
6 large eggs
¼ cup sliced green onion

1. Preheat oven to 400°. Place Tater Tots on a rimmed baking sheet, and bake for 15 minutes. Remove from oven.

2. Reduce oven temperature to 350°. Lightly grease a 13x9-inch baking dish with cooking spray.

3. In a large nonstick skillet, cook bacon over medium-high heat until crispy, 8 to 10 minutes. Remove bacon, reserving 2 tablespoons drippings in skillet; let drain on paper towels.

4. In same skillet, add sausage, onion, and chiles; cook and crumble until sausage is cooked through, 8 to 10 minutes. Stir in 1 tablespoon pepper and garlic powder. Slowly sprinkle flour into sausage mixture, and cook for 1 to 2 minutes. Slowly add 2 cups half-and-half, stirring constantly. Bring to a simmer, and cook, stirring constantly, until thickened, about 2 minutes. Pour mixture into prepared baking dish. Sprinkle with 1½ cups cheese. Place cooked Tater Tots in a single layer on top of cheese.

5. Whisk together eggs, remaining ¼ teaspoon pepper, and remaining 2 tablespoons half-and-half until frothy. Pour mixture evenly over Tater Tots. Sprinkle with remaining 1½ cups cheese.

6. Bake until set, about 35 to 40 minutes. Sprinkle with cooked bacon and green onion. Serve warm.

HOT TIP: For step 5, I use a blender bottle to scramble the eggs. You can add the remaining pepper and remaining half-and-half to the blender bottle and then pour the mixture over the top of the Tater Tots.

Stuffed Breakfast Shells

Makes 8 servings

Who says pasta is only for lunch or dinner? This is a breakfast of champions right here!

1	pound bacon
3	medium russet potatoes, peeled and diced
1½	teaspoons kosher salt, divided
1½	teaspoons ground black pepper, divided
½	teaspoon garlic powder
¼	teaspoon cayenne pepper
1	tablespoon unsalted butter
6	large eggs, lightly beaten
1	pound ground breakfast sausage
⅓	cup all-purpose flour
2	cups half-and-half (or whole milk)
1	(8-ounce) package finely shredded triple-Cheddar cheese blend
1	(8-ounce) box manicotti pasta shells, cooked according to package directions
	Pepper Belly Pete's Zippy-Zap Sauce, to serve

1. Preheat oven to 350°. Lightly grease a 13x9-inch baking dish with cooking spray.

2. In large cast-iron skillet, cook bacon over medium heat until crispy, 4 to 5 minutes. Remove bacon and let drain on paper towels, reserving drippings in skillet. Crumble bacon.

3. Cook potatoes in bacon drippings over medium-high heat. Stir in 1 teaspoon salt, ½ teaspoon black pepper, garlic powder, and cayenne pepper. Cook until golden brown and tender, 10 to 15 minutes; let drain on paper towel.

4. Heat a large nonstick skillet over medium heat. Melt butter. Add eggs, and cook, stirring constantly, until eggs are just set, 4 to 5 minutes. Remove from skillet; set aside. Wipe skillet clean.

5. In the same skillet, add sausage; cook and crumble over medium heat until sausage is cooked through, 8 to 10 minutes. Stir in remaining ½ teaspoon salt and remaining 1 teaspoon black pepper. Slowly stir in flour until well combined, and cook for about 1 minute more. Slowly stir in half-and-half. Reduce heat to low, and simmer, stirring constantly, until thick and bubbly, about 4 to 5 minutes. Remove from heat.

6. In a large bowl, combine bacon, potatoes, eggs, and cheese. Spoon mixture evenly into pasta shells. Place in prepared dish. Pour sausage gravy over pasta shells.

7. Bake until bubbly, about 30 minutes. Serve warm with Zippy-Zap Sauce, if desired.

S.O.S.
Makes 8 servings

WATCH MY RECIPE VIDEO HERE.

**I had this recipe at least once a week when I was growing up.
My father brought it back from the army back in the 1960s.**

1½ **pounds ground beef**
½ **cup chopped white onion**
2 **teaspoons kosher salt**
2 **teaspoons garlic powder**
2 **teaspoons ground black pepper**
¼ **cup all-purpose flour**
2 **cups whole milk**
½ **(10.5-ounce) can cream of mushroom soup**
16 **slices white bread, to serve (1 whole loaf white bread)**

1. In a medium nonstick skillet, cook beef over medium-high heat until beef is medium (some pink remains); drain the grease. Add onion, salt, garlic powder, and pepper; cook until onion is softened and meat is cooked through, 4 to 5 minutes more. Reduce heat to medium-low. Slowly stir in flour until well combined. Slowly stir in milk and soup. Reduce heat to low, and bring to a simmer, stirring constantly, until desired thickness, 10 to 15 minutes.
2. Serve mixture on top of bread slices.

My dad and mom (Norman and Cathy) in Hot Springs, Arkansas, during a summer vacation.

HOT TIP: This recipe can also be served over mashed potatoes.

Sausage Bread

Makes 6 servings

My wife's family loves this hearty recipe, especially in the winter.

1 **(16-ounce) loaf self-rising white bread dough*, frozen**
1 **pound ground breakfast sausage**
1 **(4-ounce) can diced Hatch green chiles**
2 **cups shredded mozzarella cheese**
2 **large eggs, beaten**

1. Place bread dough on a plate. Cover and let stand in a warm, draft-free place (75°) until thawed and doubled in size, about 8 hours or overnight.

2. In a medium nonstick skillet, cook sausage over medium-high heat until browned, 6 to 8 minutes. Let drain on paper towels.

3. Preheat oven to 350°. Line a rimmed baking pan with foil, and lightly grease with cooking spray.

4. In a medium bowl, mix together cooked sausage and green chiles until combined.

5. Place a sheet of wax paper on the countertop and spray with cooking spray. Using your hands, stretch thawed dough into an 18x10-inch rectangle. Spread sausage mixture down the middle of the bread dough, leaving a 2-inch border on long sides of dough. Sprinkle with mozzarella cheese, and pour eggs on top.

6. Starting at one long side, pull long sides up and over filling, meeting in the middle and pinching seam to seal. Then pinch ends together until well sealed. Carefully lift off wax paper, and place, seam side down, on prepared pan.

7. Bake until lightly golden brown, 25 minutes. Serve warm.

*I use Rhodes Bake-N-Serv® White Bread.

Rojo Breakfast Burrito

Makes 2

If breakfast is the most important meal of the day, then you might as well do it right! Give this bad boy a try!

1   (12-ounce) package fresh chorizo sausage, casings removed
4   small red potatoes, chopped
1   fresh jalapeño, chopped
¼   cup chopped red onion
½   cup water
1   tablespoon unsalted butter
3   large eggs, lightly beaten
¼   teaspoon kosher salt
¼   teaspoon ground black pepper
3   tablespoons ranch dressing
1   tablespoon Sriracha sauce
2   burrito-size tortillas
½   cup grated habanero Cheddar cheese*
2   tablespoons chipotle pepper sauce*

1. In a 10-inch cast-iron skillet, add sausage; cook and crumble over medium-high heat until sausage is cooked through, 8 to 10 minutes. Add potatoes, jalapeño, and onion. Stir in ½ cup water, cover, and cook over medium-low heat until potatoes are tender, about 15 minutes. Remove from heat and stir.
2. Heat a 10-inch nonstick skillet over medium heat. Melt butter, add eggs, and cook, stirring constantly, until eggs are just set. Add salt and black pepper. Remove from heat.
3. In a small bowl, mix together ranch and Sriracha.
4. Divide sausage mixture evenly onto each tortilla, and top evenly with eggs and cheese. Drizzle each with ranch-Sriracha sauce; tuck in sides and roll up. Brush outside of burritos with chipotle pepper sauce. Serve immediately.

I use Cabot Wickedly Habanero Cheddar Cheese and Tobasco Chipotle Pepper Sauce.

Breakfast Pizza

Makes 1 (16-inch) pizza

Everybody likes pizza! If you're in a breakfast rut at your house, give this recipe a try.

1   pound ground breakfast sausage
1   small white onion, diced
2   teaspoons kosher salt, divided
2   teaspoons ground black pepper, divided
1½   teaspoons garlic powder
¼   cup all-purpose flour
2   cups whole milk
12   large eggs
1½   tablespoons unsalted butter
2   (8-ounce) cans refrigerated crescent roll dough
1   pound bacon, cooked and crumbled
1   (8-ounce) package shredded Mexican cheese blend

1. Preheat oven to 375°. Lightly grease a 16-inch pizza pan with cooking spray.

2. In a medium nonstick skillet, cook sausage over medium-high heat until cooked through, 7 to 8 minutes; drain the grease. Add onion, 1½ teaspoons salt, 1½ teaspoons pepper, and garlic powder; cook until onions are softened, 3 to 4 minutes. Slowly stir in flour until well combined, and cook for about 1 minute more. Slowly stir in milk. Reduce heat to low, and simmer, stirring constantly, until thick and bubbly, about 15 minutes. Remove from heat, and let cool slightly.

3. In a medium bowl, lightly beat eggs; beat in remaining ½ teaspoon salt and remaining ½ teaspoon pepper until frothy, 1 to 2 minutes.

4. In a large nonstick skillet, heat butter over medium heat; cook beaten eggs, stirring often, until eggs are cooked but still wet. Remove from heat; set aside.

5. Unroll crescent roll dough, and place on prepared pan with points of dough toward the center. Pinch together all seams between dough to make one crust. Around outside edge, roll down the top of each crescent, one turn each, pressing to seal, to form crust.

6. Bake until golden brown, 10 to 15 minutes.

7. Reduce oven temperature to 350°. Spoon sausage mixture evenly over cooked crescent roll crust. Sprinkle eggs and bacon evenly on top. Sprinkle with cheese.

8. Bake until cheese is melted, 10 minutes more. Serve warm.

Homemade Biscuits and Country Gravy

Makes 8 servings

If you learn to make one recipe, it should be homemade biscuits. Teach your kids and grandkids how to make them, too. And, hey, adding gravy on top can't hurt.

HOMEMADE BISCUITS
¼   **cup plus 1 teaspoon vegetable shortening, divided**
2¼   **cups scooped self-rising flour**
1   **cup whole buttermilk**
Unsalted butter, melted

COUNTRY GRAVY
½   **cup bacon grease**
¾   **cup all-purpose flour**
1   **teaspoon kosher salt**
1   **teaspoon ground black pepper**
4   **cups whole milk**
Topping: ground black pepper

1. For biscuits: Preheat oven to 500°. Grease a 10-inch cast-iron skillet with 1 teaspoon shortening.
2. In a medium bowl, add self-rising flour and remaining ¼ cup shortening. Using your hands, combine flour and shortening until shortening is mixed into flour and there are no lumps, about 5 minutes.

3. Make a well in center of flour, and slowly add in buttermilk, stirring with your hands to incorporate, about 5 minutes. (Dough should hold its shape in a disk.)
4. Place on a well-floured surface. With floured hands, fold dough at least 4 to 5 times. Press into ½-inch thickness. Using your hands, tear and shape into 8 (3-inch) round biscuits. Place in prepared pan, making sure they touch.
5. Bake until golden brown, 10 to 12 minutes. Brush tops with butter as desired.
6. For gravy: In a large cast-iron skillet, heat bacon grease over medium heat. Whisk in flour, and cook, whisking constantly, until golden brown, 2 to 3 minutes. Whisk in salt and pepper. Slowly whisk in milk. Cook, whisking constantly, until thickened and bubbly, 6 to 8 minutes. Serve hot gravy over biscuits. Top with pepper, if desired.

HOT TIP: If you don't have a biscuit cutter, use an empty can or cookie cutter. Or you can use your hands and tear off biscuit-size sections. They don't have to be perfect—they just need to taste good!

Farmer's Favorite Breakfast Casserole

Makes about 8 servings

This is a recipe my mother cooked when I was growing up. She saved it for weekends whenever we had family visiting from out of town.

12   large eggs
3   cups shredded Colby-Jack cheese blend
½   cup sour cream
½   cup whole milk
3   tablespoons unsalted butter
2   pounds ground breakfast sausage
2   cups chopped yellow onion
1   cup chopped fresh jalapeño
1   teaspoon garlic powder
1   teaspoon ground black pepper

1. Preheat oven to 350°. Lightly grease a 13x9-inch baking dish with cooking spray.
2. In a large bowl, whisk eggs, cheese, sour cream, and milk until incorporated.
3. In a large nonstick skillet, melt butter over medium-high heat. Add sausage, onion, jalapeño, garlic powder, and black pepper. Cook and crumble sausage until sausage is cooked through and vegetables are tender, about 15 minutes. Drain well. Stir sausage mixture into egg mixture. Pour into prepared pan.
4. Bake until set, 45 to 55 minutes. Cut into squares. Serve warm.

Tim Murdock (my first cousin), my grandmother (Nelly), and me. This was taken at my birthday party when I was about 16. I had these sideburns because of a bet, and this photo has haunted me ever since!

CHAPTER 2

TAILGATING APPS

NEXT TIME EVERYBODY SHOWS UP AT YOUR HOUSE FOR THE BIG GAME, BE READY WITH SOME OF THESE SNACKS. THE ONLY PROBLEM IS, THOSE FOLKS ARE GOING TO KEEP SHOWING BACK UP EVERY WEEK AFTER THAT.

Chuck Wagon Wheels

Makes about 24

This recipe will have you throwing rocks at regular onion rings.
Once you try these, you won't go back.

3	large white onions, sliced ½ inch thick
1½	pounds fresh ground chuck
8	buttery round crackers*, crushed
2	cups shredded Colby-Jack cheese blend
Thinly sliced bacon (about 2½ pounds)	

1. If preheating is recommended by your air fryer's instruction manual, preheat fryer to 400°.

2. Sort through onion slices and set aside about 24 large onion slices and about 24 smaller onion slices. The smaller slices should be about 1 inch wide through the middle.

3. In a medium bowl, add ground chuck, crackers, and cheese; using hands, mix until well combined.

4. Take 1 large raw onion ring and pack about 3 tablespoons filling around the inner edges. Take a small raw onion ring and press it into the center of the filled ring so the finished product resembles a wheel. Repeat with remaining raw onion rings and remaining filling.

5. Wrap each onion wheel with about 2 to 3 slices of bacon, trimming any excess.

6. Working in batches, place wheels in air fryer (if preheating is not recommended, set temperature to 400°), and air fry until browned and crisp, about 20 minutes, rearranging wheels halfway. Drain excess bacon drippings between batches. Let drain on paper towels. Serve immediately.

*I use Ritz Crackers.

Fried Cheese Balls

Makes about 15

If you make this recipe when you're having folks over to watch the game, you're going to be the MVP every time!

1   **pound ground beef**
1   **fresh jalapeño, diced**
1   **cup chopped sweet onion**
1   **teaspoon garlic powder**
1   **teaspoon cayenne pepper**
1   **teaspoon ground black pepper**
1   **(10-ounce) can hot diced tomatoes with habaneros, drained well**
1   **(8-ounce) package cream cheese**
1   **(16-ounce) block Mexican processed cheese product*, cubed**
1   **tablespoon Pepper Belly Pete's Zippy-Zap Sauce**
2   **cups shredded Colby-Jack cheese blend**
1   **(8-ounce) block part-skim mozzarella cheese, cut into ¾-inch cubes**
Vegetable oil, for frying
6   **large eggs**
7   **tablespoons all-purpose flour**
1½   **(9.75-ounce) bags hot tortilla chips*, finely crushed**

DIPPING SAUCE
1   **cup ranch dressing**
1   **tablespoon Pepper Belly Pete's Zippy-Zap Sauce**

1. In a large Dutch oven, combine ground beef, jalapeño, onion, garlic powder, cayenne pepper, and black pepper. Cook and crumble over medium-high heat until meat is cooked through, 8 to 10 minutes. Stir in diced tomatoes, cream cheese, processed cheese, and Zippy-Zap Sauce, and cook over medium-low heat until everything is melted. Remove from heat, and let cool.

2. Stir in Colby-Jack cheese. Use hands to flatten about ⅓ cup beef mixture into patties. Place 1 cube mozzarella in center of each patty, and fold the mixture around it; shape into a ball. Repeat with remaining beef mixture and remaining mozzarella cubes. Place on a baking sheet greased with cooking spray, and freeze for about 2 hours.

3. In a large Dutch oven, fill halfway with oil. Heat oil over medium-high heat until a deep-fry thermometer registers 350°. Line a baking sheet with paper towels.

4. In a medium bowl, whisk together eggs and flour.

5. In another medium bowl, place crushed tortilla chips.

6. Take balls out of freezer, and remove from baking sheet using a spatula. Dip each ball in egg mixture, letting excess drip off, and then roll in chips to coat.

7. Working in batches, carefully drop cheese balls into hot oil (don't overfill pot). Fry until crispy, 3 to 4 minutes. Remove with a slotted spoon, and let drain on prepared pan.

8. For dipping sauce: In a small bowl, stir together ranch dressing and Zippy-Zap Sauce. Serve warm with cheese balls.

*I use Velveeta Mexican and Doritos Flamin' Hot Cool Ranch tortilla chips.

WATCH MY RECIPE VIDEO HERE.

Chicken Wing Poppers

Makes 16

Chicken wings are hard to beat, but these Chicken Wing Poppers will win the race every time!

5   **pounds chicken wings**
1   **(8-ounce) package cream cheese, softened**
5   **slices bacon, cooked and crumbled (about ½ cup)**
2   **fresh jalapeños, diced**
1   **teaspoon garlic powder**
1   **teaspoon cayenne pepper**
1   **teaspoon ground black pepper**
1   **tablespoon Pepper Belly Pete's Zippy-Zap Sauce**
Olive oil, for brushing
Cajun seasoning*, to taste

1. If preheating is recommended by your air fryer's instruction manual, preheat fryer to 400°.
2. Using a sharp knife, remove the drumettes at the joint, leaving the flat and wing tip together. Cut tendons from tops of flats. Using your fingers at the top of the bone, push down on meat, stripping it from bone. Brake the two bones away from wing tip right at joint and remove, making sure not to tear through skin.
3. In a medium bowl, add cream cheese, bacon, jalapeños, garlic powder, cayenne pepper, and black pepper, folding together until well combined; stir in Zippy-Zap Sauce.
4. Stuff 1 tablespoon mixture into each boneless chicken wing. Brush each wing with a light coating of oil, and season with Cajun seasoning to taste.
5. Working in batches, place stuffed wings inside air fryer with popper opening facing up (if preheating is not recommended, set temperature to 400°), and air-fry until internal temperature is 165°, 15 to 20 minutes. Serve immediately.

*I use Cajun Two-Step.

HOT TIP: The drumettes can be fried up or air-fried as usual and drenched in hot sauce. Then you've got wings two ways, and there ain't nothing wrong with that.

Fuzzy Navel Drink

**This drink from the 1980s will have everybody dancing at your next cookout.
Be sure to label it and keep it out of reach of minors!**

Cooler:
Makes 52 servings

10	pounds ice, plus more to serve
2	gallons orange juice or orange drink
1	gallon vodka
1	(750-milliliter) bottle peach schnapps

Pepper Belly Pete's Zippy-Zap Sauce,
to serve

1. In a 5-gallon cooler, combine ice, orange juice, vodka, and peach schnapps. Serve over ice and with a dash Zippy-Zap Sauce, if desired.

Pitcher:
Makes 8 servings

1½	pounds ice, plus more to serve
5	cups orange juice or orange drink
2½	cups vodka
½	cup peach schnapps

Pepper Belly Pete's Zippy-Zap Sauce,
to serve

1. In a pitcher, combine ice, orange juice, vodka, and peach schnapps. Serve over ice and with a dash of Zippy-Zap Sauce, if desired.

Salisbury Sliders

Makes 10 servings

No grill needed for this indoor burger that packs a lot of flavor punch.

1½ pounds ground beef
10 buttery round crackers*, crushed
½ cup shredded Monterey Jack cheese with peppers
1 fresh jalapeño, grated
½ medium white onion, grated
2 large cloves garlic, grated
2 teaspoons Worcestershire sauce
½ teaspoon kosher salt
½ teaspoon ground black pepper
10 small buns, buttered and toasted
5 (1-ounce) slices Monterey Jack cheese with peppers, halved
10 tomato slices
Pepper Belly Pete's Zippy-Zap Sauce, to serve
10 pieces romaine lettuce

1. Preheat oven to 375°. Place an oven-safe wire rack (or a pizza pan with holes in the bottom) on a rimmed baking sheet. (This keeps the burgers from sitting in grease while they cook.)
2. In a large bowl, stir together ground beef, crackers, shredded cheese, jalapeño, onion, garlic, Worcestershire, salt, and black pepper. Divide mixture into 10 portions, and shape each portion into a 3-inch patty.
3. Place patties on prepared baking sheet.
4. Bake until internal temperature is 165°, 20 to 25 minutes.
5. To assemble, place 1 patty on bottom half of bun; top with 1 cheese slice half, 1 tomato slice, Zippy-Zap Sauce, and lettuce. Top with top half of bun. Repeat with remaining patties, buns, cheese slices, tomato slices, Zippy-Zap Sauce, and lettuce. Serve warm.

*I use Ritz Crackers.

HOT TIP: You can substitute bell pepper if jalapeño is too hot for you.

Spending time with Wylie around Christmas.

Nacho Chicken Wings

Makes 18 to 20

What's better than regular nachos?
Nachos built on top of air-fried chicken wings, that's what.

2   **pounds chicken wings**
2   **tablespoons olive oil**
2   **tablespoons taco seasoning**
8   **ounces tortilla chips, crushed**
Pico de gallo and white queso,
     to serve

1. If preheating is recommended by your air fryer's instruction manual, preheat fryer to 350°.
2. In a large bowl, add chicken wings, oil, and taco seasoning; toss to combine. Pour crushed tortilla chips over chicken wings, and mix until well coated.
3. Spray rack of air fryer with cooking spray. Working in batches, place chicken in air fryer (if preheating is not recommended, set temperature to 350°), and air-fry until brown and crisp and internal temperature is 165°, 25 to 30 minutes. Serve hot with pico de gallo and queso, if desired.

My birthday party around the time I was turning 5 or 6. My friend Russell was sitting next to me. We were buddies all throughout high school.

Fried Potato Balls

Makes about 28

**This is a great appetizer to try for your next cookout.
Everyone's going to be asking you for the recipe.**

4 to 5 medium russet potatoes
(about 3 pounds)
¼ cup unsalted butter
1 cup cooked and crumbled bacon
1 cup chopped green onion
1½ teaspoons kosher salt
1½ teaspoons ground black pepper
1 teaspoon garlic powder
1 teaspoon cayenne pepper
1 cup shredded mild Cheddar
cheese
½ cup half-and-half, room
temperature
Vegetable oil, for frying
1 (8-ounce) block part-skim
mozzarella cheese, cut into
about ½-inch cubes
4 large eggs
1½ tablespoons all-purpose flour
5 cups crushed baked cheese
crackers*
Pepper Belly Pete's Zippy-Zap Sauce,
to serve

1. In a medium stockpot, add potatoes and water to cover by 2 inches. Bring to a boil over high heat; cook until potatoes are tender, about 40 minutes. Drain well, and transfer to a large bowl. Add butter, bacon, green onion, salt, black pepper, garlic powder, cayenne pepper, Cheddar cheese, and half-and-half. With a potato masher, or spatula, mash potato mixture until well combined.

2. In a large Dutch oven, fill halfway with oil. Heat oil over medium-high heat until a deep-fry thermometer registers 350°. Line a baking sheet with paper towels.

3. Use hands to flatten about 3 tablespoons of potato mixture each into 3½-inch patties. Place 1 cube mozzarella in the center of each patty, and fold the mixture around it; shape into a ball. Repeat with remaining potato mixture and remaining mozzarella.

4. In a medium bowl, whisk together eggs and flour.

5. In another medium bowl, add crushed crackers.

6. Coat potato balls in egg mixture, and then roll in crushed crackers. Repeat process once more for each ball.

7. Working in batches, carefully drop potato balls into hot oil (don't overfill pot). Fry until crisp and golden, 2 to 3 minutes. Let drain on prepared pan. Serve warm with hot sauce, if desired.

I use Cheez-It Baked Snack Crackers.

Walking Taco Salad

Makes 4 servings

This recipe is great for any party. And best of all, no plates or bowl required. Your friends and family can eat right out of their own individual bags (forks might be necessary, though).

4   **(1-ounce) bags original corn chips* or chili cheese flavor, divided**

4   **cups Award-Winning Texas Chili, warmed and divided (recipe on page 177)**

2   **cups nacho Cheddar cheese sauce, warmed and divided**

½   **cup sliced fresh jalapeño, divided**

½   **cup chopped white onion, divided**

Pepper Belly Pete's Zippy-Zap Sauce, to serve

1. Cut one corner off the top and one corner off the bottom (on the same side) of 1 corn chip bag, and then cut along the long side of bag between the two cut corners. Open bag, and add about 1 cup chili, ½ cup cheese, 2 tablespoons sliced jalapeño, and 2 tablespoons onion. Repeat with remaining corn chip bags, chili, cheese, jalapeño, and onion. Serve with Zippy-Zap Sauce, if desired.

*I use Fritos Original Corn Chips.

HOT TIP: If you don't have any excess chili lying around (maybe you got hungry and ate it all), you can use store-bought canned chili with beans.

Pasta Poppers

Makes 9 servings

**This stuffed pasta shell recipe is sure to be a hit.
Trust me, it's a good one right here.**

Vegetable oil, for frying
8   slices bacon, cooked and crumbled
4   fresh jalapeños, diced
1½   teaspoons garlic powder
3½   tablespoons Pepper Belly Pete's Zippy-Zap Sauce, divided
1   (8-ounce) package cream cheese, softened
1   (8-ounce) package shredded smoked mozzarella cheese
9   manicotti pasta shells, cooked according to package directions
1   cup cornstarch
3   large eggs, beaten
1   (9.75-ounce) bag nacho cheese tortilla chips*, crushed
½   cup ranch dressing

1. In a large Dutch oven, fill halfway with oil. Heat oil over medium-high heat until a deep-fry thermometer registers 350°. Line a baking sheet with paper towels.
2. In a large bowl, combine bacon, jalapeños, garlic powder, 2 tablespoons Zippy-Zap Sauce, cream cheese, and mozzarella.
3. Cut pasta shells in half crosswise, and divide filling evenly along pasta shells.
4. In a medium bowl, add cornstarch.
5. In another medium bowl, add eggs.
6. In another medium bowl, add tortilla chips.
7. Dredge each stuffed pasta shell in cornstarch, shaking off any extra. Then dip in egg mixture, letting excess drip off. Dredge in tortilla chips.
8. Working in batches, fry pasta until crispy, 2½ minutes. Remove with a slotted spoon, and let drain on prepared pan.
9. In a small bowl, mix together ranch dressing and remaining 1½ tablespoons Zippy-Zap Sauce, and serve with stuffed pasta.

I use Doritos Nacho Cheese tortilla chips.

Fried Cheese Sticks

Makes 12

These things will have your taste buds dancing.

CHEESE STICKS

12   **(6-inch) wooden skewers**
12   **logs string cheese**
4   **large eggs**
3   **tablespoons self-rising or all-purpose flour**
1   **teaspoon garlic powder**
1   **teaspoon cayenne pepper**
½   **teaspoon ground black pepper**
1   **(8-ounce) bag spicy cheese puffs*, finely crushed**
Vegetable oil, for frying

DIPPING SAUCE

1   **cup ranch dressing**
1   **tablespoon Pepper Belly Pete's Zippy-Zap Sauce**

1. For cheese sticks: Slide 1 skewer, vertically, halfway through each string cheese log, trimming skewers to fit skillet, if necessary. (Skewers are optional). Place on a rimmed baking sheet or paper plate. Cover and freeze for 2 hours.

2. In a shallow dish, whisk together eggs, flour, garlic powder, cayenne pepper, and black pepper.

3. In another shallow dish, add crushed cheese puffs.

4. Working with 6 cheese logs at a time, roll each cheese log in egg wash until well-coated and then in crushed cheese puffs. Complete this process twice per cheese log.

5. In a 12-inch cast-iron skillet, heat ½ inch vegetable oil over medium-high heat.

6. Working in batches of 6, fry for 1 to 2 minutes per batch, turning halfway through. Drain on paper towels.

7. For dipping sauce: In a small bowl, stir together ranch dressing and Zippy-Zap Sauce. Cover and refrigerate until ready to use. Serve with warm cheese sticks.

I use CHEETOS® Puffs Flamin' Hot Cheese Flavored Snacks or CHEETOS® Crunchy Cheddar Jalapeño Cheese Flavored Snacks.

STEP-BY-STEP

These Fried Cheese Sticks are pretty easy to whip up. I let Wylie help me with these—he likes crushing the cheese puffs! Give 'em a try and see what you think.

1. After you've got your cheese on skewers, whisk your eggs, flour, garlic powder, cayenne pepper, and black pepper together.

2. Crush up your cheese puffs on a shallow plate. Eight-year-olds are especially good at this.

3. Dip your cheese stick in the egg wash. Make sure to coat it good on all sides.

4. Roll your cheese stick in the crushed cheese puffs. You want a good spicy coating on there.

5. Repeat steps 3 and 4. You want to dip it in the egg wash again and then roll it in the crushed cheese puffs again. This is going to make it extra crunchy.

6. Fry up your cheese sticks in oil. They need to cook for 1 to 2 minutes—turn 'em halfway through. After they cool a bit, serve 'em with dipping sauce.

I do a lot of frying. I know it may not be the healthiest thing, but sometimes good Southern food just needs to be fried. I wouldn't recommend eating fried foods every day, but when you do, there are a few things to keep in mind.

TAKE IT OUTSIDE

Now, this may not be a big deal to some folks, but I don't love the way frying makes my house smell. I like to fry things out on my patio, when possible. If you've got an outdoor burner, it's a great option for frying to keep your house smelling better.

COOK IN BATCHES

Overcrowding the skillet or pot can lower the temperature of the oil too much and even lead to food sticking together. Work in batches, if you need to, to make sure all of the food is cooked correctly.

KEEP IT WARM

If you are working in batches, you might be worried that your first batch will get cold while your others are cooking. I like to turn the oven on at around 225° and put batches of fried food on lined sheet pans to stay warm until it's time to eat.

DON'T BE A DUMMY

Do not pour your used oil down your sink drain. Most people know this, but I had to add it just in case. It can clog your pipe and cause a lot of headaches down the road. Some people clean and reuse their oil, and other folks wait for it to cool pour it outside or into a container and then toss it in the garbage can. Either option works—just don't pour it down the drain.

Texas Trash

Makes 12 cups

This recipe might be considered the king of all party foods. The homemade version is way better than anything you can buy in a sack.

2   **cups pretzel sticks**
2   **cups mixed nuts**
2   **cups snack mix***
2   **cups crispy corn cereal squares**
2   **cups crispy wheat cereal squares**
2   **cups crispy rice cereal squares**
1½ **cups baked cheese crackers**
¾   **cup unsalted butter**
½   **cup Worcestershire sauce**
1   **tablespoon Pepper Belly Pete's Zippy-Zap Sauce**
2   **teaspoons garlic powder**
2   **teaspoons seasoned salt**
1   **teaspoon onion powder**

1. Preheat oven to 250°.
2. In a large baking pan, combine pretzels, nuts, snack mix, cereal squares, and cheese crackers.
3. In a medium skillet, melt butter over medium heat; stir in Worcestershire, Zippy-Zap Sauce, garlic powder, seasoned salt, and onion powder; cook, stirring constantly, until well combined. Pour slowly over pretzel mixture, stirring constantly to coat.
4. Bake until browned and fragrant, 1 hour to 1 hour and 15 minutes, stirring every 15 minutes.

I use Gardetto's Original Recipe Snack Mix.

Sara, Wylie, and me getting ready to have friends over for a cookout.

CHAPTER 3

GAME DAY
DIPS

GRAB A TORTILLA CHIP AND GET READY TO DIP. YOUR TASTE BUDS ARE ABOUT TO THANK YOU.

Loaded Bean Dip

Makes about 12 servings

This one right here is extra tasty when it's cold outside. It's almost guaranteed to keep you warm and full.

1 pound ground breakfast sausage
1 (1-ounce) package taco seasoning
1 (16-ounce) can refried beans
½ cup hot taco sauce*
2 tablespoons half-and-half
1 (10-ounce) can fire-roasted diced tomatoes with green chiles
1 (10-ounce) package queso quesadilla cheese, grated
1 (16-ounce) round ball Oaxaca cheese, shredded
Toppings: finely chopped tomatoes, sliced black olives, chopped fresh cilantro
Tortilla chips and fried pork rinds, to serve

1. Preheat smoker to 225°.
2. In a 12-inch cast-iron skillet, cook and crumble sausage over medium-high heat until brown, about 8 to 10 minutes. Stir in taco seasoning, and cook until heated through, 1 to 2 minutes more. Remove from skillet, and let drain on paper towels. Wipe skillet clean.
3. In the same skillet, cook beans over medium heat until heated through, about 2 to 3 minutes. Stir in taco sauce and half-and-half; remove from heat. Using a spatula, spread into a thin layer. Top with cooked sausage mixture.
4. In a medium microwave-safe bowl, add tomatoes and queso cheese. Heat on high for 2 minutes until cheese is melted, stirring halfway through. Pour cheese mixture evenly over sausage. Sprinkle with Oaxaca cheese.
5. Cook in smoker until cheese melts and is lightly golden brown, about 1 hour. Top with tomatoes, olives, and cilantro, if desired. Serve immediately with tortilla chips and pork rinds.

*I use Ortega Taco Sauce Original Thick and Smooth (hot).

HOT TIP: You can bake this in the oven if you don't have a smoker. Just preheat your broiler and make the dip using steps 2 through 4. Broil it in your skillet on the middle rack of the oven until the cheese melts and begins to brown, just about 2 to 3 minutes.

Bacon Cheeseburger Dip

Makes about 18 servings

Once you put some of this Bacon Cheeseburger Dip on a chip, you won't be able to stop going back for more.

10   slices bacon, cooked and crumbled
2   pounds ground beef, cooked and crumbled
3   fresh jalapeños, chopped
2   cups diced fresh tomatoes
1   large white onion, chopped
2   tablespoons minced garlic
2   tablespoons Cajun seasoning*
1   (12-ounce) can evaporated milk
2   tablespoons Worcestershire sauce
2   tablespoons Pepper Belly Pete's Zippy-Zap Sauce
1   (16-ounce) block medium Cheddar cheese, cubed
1   (16-ounce) block Monterey Jack cheese with peppers, cubed
1   (8-ounce) package cream cheese, cubed and softened
Toppings: chopped fresh jalapeño
Tortilla chips, to serve

1. In a 6-quart slow cooker, combine bacon, beef, jalapeños, tomatoes, onion, garlic, Cajun seasoning, evaporated milk, Worcestershire, Zippy-Zap Sauce, cheeses, and cream cheese. Cover with lid, and cook on low until cheese is melted and smooth, about 2 hours to 2 hours and 30 minutes, stirring every 30 minutes. Top with jalapeño, if desired. Serve with tortilla chips.

*I use Cajun Two-Step.

Guacamole

Makes 7 cups

I call this "the best salad ever." Have you ever had another salad this good?
I bet not.

5   seedless tomatoes, chopped
4   avocados, peeled, pitted, and
    chopped
3   fresh jalapeños, chopped
1   medium white onion, chopped
1   cup chopped fresh cilantro
4   cloves garlic, minced
1   teaspoon kosher salt
½   teaspoon ground black pepper
½   cup fresh lime juice (about
    3 limes)
Tortilla chips, to serve

1. In a large bowl, add tomatoes, avocados, jalapeños, onion, cilantro, garlic, salt, black pepper, and lime juice; using a fork or potato masher, smash until combined. Serve immediately with tortilla chips.

Queso Verde

Makes about 14 servings

When you add tomatillo salsa to your queso, your friends are going to be green with envy. Might as well invite them all over to eat it with you.

3   tablespoons unsalted butter
1   cup roughly chopped fresh cilantro
1   (16-ounce) jar Pepper Belly Pete's Hot Tomatillo Avocado Salsa
1   (12-ounce) can evaporated milk
2   cups shredded sharp white Cheddar cheese
1½   cups shredded Monterey Jack cheese with peppers
1½   cups half-and-half
Toppings: chopped fresh cilantro
Tortilla chips, to serve

1. In a large nonstick skillet, add butter, cilantro, salsa, evaporated milk, and cheeses. Cook over medium-low heat, stirring constantly, until cheese is melted, about 10 to 12 minutes. Stir in half-and-half, and cook until steaming. Top with cilantro, if desired. Serve immediately with tortilla chips.

This is me on a family vacation posing on the Texas border, probably coming in from Arkansas.

WATCH MY RECIPE VIDEO HERE.

Birria Chicken Dip

Makes 18 to 22 servings

As soon as your friends and family smell this dip cooking, they're going to be drooling everywhere. You might need to hand out bibs at the door.

3 boneless skinless chicken breasts (2 to 2½ pounds)
8 guajillo chiles, stemmed and seeded
5 chile de árbol, stemmed and seeded
4 dried ancho chiles, stemmed and seeded
1 (4-ounce) can chipotle peppers with adobo sauce
8 large cloves garlic
4 plum tomatoes, coarsely chopped
1 large yellow onion, chopped
1½ teaspoons kosher salt
1½ teaspoons dried Mexican oregano
1½ teaspoons ground cumin
1½ teaspoons whole black peppercorns
3 dried bay leaves
1 (4-inch) cinnamon stick
4 cups chicken stock
1 (32-ounce) block Monterey Jack cheese with peppers, cubed
1 (16-ounce) block quesadilla cheese, cubed
1 (12-ounce) can evaporated milk
2 tablespoons Pepper Belly Pete's Zippy-Zap Sauce
Tortilla chips, to serve

1. In a 6-quart slow cooker, add chicken, guajillo chiles, arbol chiles, ancho chiles, chipotle peppers, garlic, tomatoes, onion, salt, oregano, cumin, peppercorns, bay leaves, cinnamon stick, and chicken stock. Cover with lid, and cook on low until chicken is fully cooked and vegetables are tender, about 4 hours.

2. Remove chicken, and using 2 forks, shred chicken. Remove bay leaves and cinnamon stick. Strain vegetables, reserving 1 cup of liquid, discarding the rest.

3. In the container of a blender, add vegetables and reserved 1 cup liquid, and process until smooth.

4. Return chicken to empty slow cooker, and top with blended sauce, stirring to combine. Stir in cheeses, evaporated milk, and Zippy-Zap Sauce. Cover with lid, and cook on low, stirring occasionally, until cheese is melted, about 1 hour. Serve warm with tortilla chips.

HOT TIP: Cut your cheeses into small cubes so they don't take too long to melt.

81

Flavor-Time Queso

Makes 12 to 14 servings

If you like cheese dip, you're really gonna like this one.
Get your chip ready.

4   plum tomatoes, seeded and chopped
4   cloves garlic, minced
2   fresh jalapeños, finely chopped
1   medium yellow onion, finely chopped
1   (8-ounce) package cream cheese, cubed and softened
1   (8-ounce) block pasteurized processed cheese product*, cubed
1   (8-ounce) block Monterey Jack cheese with peppers, cubed
1   (8-ounce) block medium Cheddar cheese, cubed
1   (12-ounce) can evaporated milk
1   tablespoon Pepper Belly Pete's Flavor-Time Sizzling Steak Sauce
Tortilla chips, to serve

1. In a 6-quart slow cooker, add tomatoes, garlic, jalapeños, onion, cream cheese, cheeses, evaporated milk, and Sizzling Steak Sauce, stirring to incorporate. Cover and cook on low, stirring occasionally, until melted, about 1 hour and 30 minutes. Serve warm with tortilla chips, if desired.

I use Velveeta Cheese.

I always enjoy spending time with Wylie.

Spinach Dip

Makes 6 to 8 servings

This right here is one of my healthy recipes. But don't worry, it still tastes great.

2   fresh jalapeños, chopped
1   (10-ounce) package frozen spinach, thawed and well drained
1   bunch green onion, chopped
2   cups full-fat Greek yogurt
1   cup sour cream
½   cup mayonnaise
1   tablespoon Pepper Belly Pete's Zippy-Zap Sauce
¾   teaspoon garlic powder
¾   teaspoon onion powder
Corn chip scoops* and fresh vegetables, to serve

1. In the container of a blender or food processor, add jalapeños, spinach, green onion, Greek yogurt, sour cream, mayonnaise, Zippy-Zap Sauce, garlic powder, and onion powder; pulse until incorporated, about 5 to 6 pulses, stopping occasionally to scrape the side of the container. Pour into a bowl. Cover and chill for at least 1 hour. Serve cold with corn chips and vegetables.

*I use Fritos® Scoops!® Corn Chips.

HOT TIP: Stir in any other seasonings or ingredients you like to make it your own. You can use any kind of chip or cracker with this dip. Or use it as a chance to get in your veggies and dip with broccoli, carrots, cauliflower, cucumbers, or anything else really—your doctor will be proud of you.

Four-Cheese Skillet Dip

Makes about 16 servings

This dip's got breakfast sausage in it, so as far as I'm concerned, you can eat it for breakfast. It'll fill you up more than an ole bowl of cereal.

1   **pound ground breakfast sausage**
1   **(10-ounce) can fire-roasted diced tomatoes with green chiles**
½   **cup heavy whipping cream**
1   **tablespoon Pepper Belly Pete's Flavor-Time Sizzling Steak Sauce**
1   **(16-ounce) package pasteurized processed cheese product*, cubed**
1   **(8-ounce) block Monterey Jack cheese with peppers, cubed**
1   **(8-ounce) block white Cheddar cheese, cubed**
1   **(8-ounce) package cream cheese, cubed**
Tortilla chips, to serve

1. In a 12-inch cast-iron skillet, cook sausage over medium-high heat until cooked and crumbled, 8 to 10 minutes. Add tomatoes, cream, Sizzling Steak Sauce, cheeses, and cream cheese. Reduce heat to low, and cook, stirring occasionally, until cheese is melted, 10 to 12 minutes. Serve hot with tortilla chips.

*I use Velveeta Cheese.

Christmas when I was about 5 years old.

CHAPTER 4

SOUPS AND
STEWS

WHEN THE WEATHER COOLS OFF,
GET OUT YOUR BIG POT AND COOK UP
ONE OF THESE SOUPS OR STEWS FOR
YOUR FAMILY. THEY'RE GONNA LOVE IT.

Taco Soup

Makes 8 to 10 servings

This is a soup that everybody loves. It's great for an easy dinner to feed the whole family any night of the week.

2½   pounds ground beef
1   medium white onion, chopped
1   large fresh jalapeño, chopped
2   teaspoons Worcestershire sauce
2   (2-ounce) packages taco seasoning mix
2   (1-ounce) packages ranch dressing mix
1   tablespoon garlic powder
1½   teaspoons ground black pepper
1   (15.3-ounce) can white hominy, drained
1   (15.25-ounce) can yellow whole kernel corn, drained
1   (15-ounce) can black beans, drained
1   (15-ounce) can Ranch Style Beans
1   (10-ounce) can diced tomatoes with green chiles
1   (32-ounce) container chicken broth
Toppings: multicolored tortilla chips, sliced avocado, shredded Cheddar-Jack cheese blend, sour cream
Pepper Belly Pete's Zippy-Zap Sauce, to serve

1. In a large Dutch oven, cook ground beef over medium-high heat, stirring frequently, until cooked through and crumbly, 6 to 8 minutes. Let drain on paper towels.

2. In same Dutch oven, cook onion, jalapeño, and Worcestershire, stirring frequently, until vegetables are tender, 3 to 4 minutes.

3. Stir in cooked meat, taco seasoning mix, ranch dressing mix, garlic powder, black pepper, hominy, corn, beans, tomatoes, and broth. Cook for 30 minutes, stirring occasionally. Top each serving with tortilla chips, avocado, cheese, and sour cream, if desired. Serve hot with Zippy-Zap Sauce, if desired.

Loaded Ancho Potato Soup

Makes 8 to 10 servings

WATCH MY RECIPE
VIDEO HERE.

It's time to bring your potato soup game to the next level with this recipe. After you add in the bacon, chili powder, and cheese, everybody in the neighborhood's gonna show up at your door asking for a bowl.

1   pound bacon, chopped
1   medium white onion, chopped
1   tablespoon Pepper Belly Pete's Zippy-Zap Sauce
1   tablespoon ground black pepper
1   teaspoon kosher salt
1   teaspoon ancho chili powder
1   teaspoon cayenne pepper
½   cup all-purpose flour
2   cups heavy whipping cream
3   cups shredded sharp white Cheddar cheese
1   (32-ounce) container chicken broth
3½   pounds russet potatoes, peeled and cubed
2   cups water
1   bunch green onion, sliced
1   teaspoon garlic powder
1   cup sour cream
Toppings: chopped cooked bacon, sour cream, sliced green onion

1. In a large Dutch oven, cook bacon over medium heat until crispy, 6 to 7 minutes. Remove from pan with slotted spoon, reserving drippings in the Dutch oven. Let drain on paper towels. Save ¼ cup bacon to go on top of soup.

2. In same Dutch oven, add onion and Zippy-Zap Sauce; cook, stirring constantly to loosen bits from bottom of pan, until onion softens, 3 to 4 minutes. Add black pepper, salt, chili powder, and cayenne pepper, and cook for about 2 to 3 minutes more. Slowly stir in flour. Cook, stirring constantly, until combined and slightly thickened, 2 to 3 minutes.

3. Slowly stir in cream and cheese, and stir until smooth. Slowly add in broth until combined. Add potatoes and 2 cups water. Cover and let simmer until potatoes are tender, about 45 minutes, stirring every 10 to 15 minutes.

4. Stir in cooked bacon, green onion, garlic powder, and sour cream; cover and cook for 20 to 25 minutes, stirring occasionally. Top each serving with saved bacon, sour cream, and green onion, if desired. Serve hot.

Green Chile Stew

Makes about 10 servings

Out of all the soups and stews, this one might be my favorite. If you haven't had Green Chile Stew before, you gotta give this one a try.

3½ pounds boneless pork country style ribs, cut into 1½-inch pieces
6 cloves garlic, minced
1½ teaspoons kosher salt, divided
1½ teaspoons ground black pepper, divided
1 tablespoon olive oil
1 large white onion, chopped
2 plum tomatoes, chopped
1 teaspoon ground cumin
1 teaspoon dried oregano
1 (16-ounce) jar Hatch green chiles*
1 (15-ounce) can green enchilada sauce
1 (12-ounce) can lager beer
1 tablespoon Pepper Belly Pete's Zippy-Zap Sauce
2 dried bay leaves
2½ pounds russet potatoes, peeled and sliced ¼ inch thick
1 (32-ounce) container chicken broth
Toppings: sour cream and fresh chopped cilantro
Pepper Belly Pete's Zippy-Zap Sauce, to serve

1. In a medium bowl, combine pork, garlic, 1 teaspoon salt, and 1 teaspoon pepper. Cover and refrigerate for 30 minutes.

2. In a large Dutch oven, heat oil over medium-high heat, and cook onion until softened, 4 to 5 minutes. Add pork; cook, stirring occasionally, until lightly browned, about 8 minutes. Stir in tomatoes, cumin, oregano, remaining ½ teaspoon salt, and remaining ½ teaspoon pepper. Stir in green chiles, enchilada sauce, beer, and Zippy-Zap Sauce. Bring to a simmer, and add bay leaves. Cook, uncovered, until pork is almost tender, about 45 minutes, stirring occasionally.

3. Stir in potatoes and broth. Cook, uncovered, until potatoes are tender and break apart, 30 to 40 minutes. Remove bay leaves. Top each serving with sour cream and cilantro, if desired. Serve hot with Zippy-Zap Sauce, if desired.

I use Zia Hatch Chile Company's Roasted New Mexico Hatch Green Chile (Medium).

Creamy Chicken Noodle Soup

Makes 8 to 10 servings

It's just like that old-timey chicken noodle soup your mama used to make, but this one's even better.

½ cup unsalted butter
4 carrots, cut into 1-inch slices
4 stalks celery, sliced
1 large white onion, chopped
1½ teaspoons poultry seasoning
1½ teaspoons smoked paprika
1½ teaspoons Cajun seasoning*
1½ teaspoons ground black pepper
1 teaspoon tomato bouillon with chicken flavor
1 tablespoon Pepper Belly Pete's Zippy-Zap Sauce
4 cups shredded rotisserie chicken
5 cloves garlic, minced
10 cups chicken stock, divided
2 cups heavy whipping cream
12 ounces freshly grated white American cheese
1 (16-ounce) package rotini pasta

1. In a large Dutch oven, melt butter over medium-high heat. Add carrots, celery, onion, poultry seasoning, paprika, Cajun seasoning, pepper, bouillon, and Zippy-Zap Sauce. Cook, stirring constantly, until vegetables are slightly softened, about 5 minutes.

2. Stir in chicken, garlic, 8 cups chicken stock, cream, and cheese, and simmer over medium heat. Cover and cook for about 15 minutes, stirring occasionally.

3. Add pasta and remaining 2 cups chicken stock, and simmer over medium heat until pasta is cooked through, stirring occasionally, about 20 minutes. Serve hot.

I use Cajun Two-Step.

This is my mom. I think she was mad at me for taking a picture when she was cleaning the house. This was some time in the early 1980s.

Sausage and Kale Soup

Makes 12 servings

There is an old saying: In life, only two things are certain; that's death and taxes. I've got another one for you. If you ever see me add kale to a dish, it will have Zippy-Zap Sauce.

2 pounds hot Italian sausage, casing removed
3 pounds russet potatoes, thinly sliced
5 cups stemmed and torn fresh kale
1 medium white onion, chopped
1 tablespoon dried Italian seasoning
1 tablespoon ground black pepper
6 cups chicken broth
6 cups water
2 cups heavy whipping cream
2 tablespoons Zippy Zap Sauce
Toppings: shredded Parmesan cheese, chopped cooked bacon

1. In a large Dutch oven, cook and crumble sausage over medium-high heat, stirring frequently, until meat is cooked through, 8 to 10 minutes. Let drain on paper towels, reserving drippings in the pan.
2. In same Dutch oven, add potatoes, kale, onion, Italian seasoning, pepper, chicken broth, and 6 cups water. Cover and cook over medium-low heat until potatoes are tender, about 30 minutes.
3. Stir in cooked sausage, cream, and Zippy-Zap Sauce and let simmer for 15 minutes. Top each serving with shredded Parmesan cheese and chopped cooked bacon, if desired. Serve hot.

HOT TIP: Make sure you remove the stalks from the kale leaves, and don't put the stalks in your soup. Wash your leaves good before you add them to the pot.

Chicken Gumbo

Makes about 8 servings

This might not be an official Cajun gumbo, but it won't steer you wrong. It's a good one.

1   **whole chicken, about 6 pounds**
2   **tablespoons Cajun seasoning*, divided**
1   **cup olive oil**
2   **cups all-purpose flour**
1   **cup chopped white onion**
1   **cup chopped celery**
1   **cup chopped green bell pepper**
1   **tablespoon minced fresh garlic**
2   **(32-ounce) containers chicken broth**
2   **pounds smoked sausage, sliced**
1   **tablespoon ground black pepper**
1   **pound frozen sliced okra, thawed**
Kosher salt, to taste
Hot cooked rice, to serve

1. Skin and debone chicken, keeping the back and neck bones, and cut meat into 1-inch chunks.

2. In a medium bowl, toss together chicken, back and neck bones, and 1 tablespoon Cajun seasoning.

3. In a large cast-iron Dutch oven, add oil. Add flour slowly, mixing well. Cook over medium-low heat, stirring constantly, until mixture is a chocolate color, 45 to 50 minutes. (If you drink beer, this is a good time to drink one, or six!)

4. Add onion, celery, bell pepper, and garlic to roux. Cook, stirring occasionally, until vegetables are softened, 3 to 5 minutes. Gradually stir in broth. Add chicken with back and neck bones, sausage, black pepper, and remaining 1 tablespoon Cajun seasoning. Cover and simmer for 3 hours, stirring occasionally. Add okra, and simmer for 1 hour, stirring occasionally, using a large wooden spatula with a flat edge to prevent sticking on the bottom. Remove back and neck bones with a slotted spoon. Add salt to taste. Serve hot with rice.

*I use Cajun Two-Step.

Beef Stew

Makes about 8 servings

Talk about warming your belly up. This is about to be your new favorite winter recipe right here.

2½ pounds chuck roast, trimmed and cut into 1-inch cubes

⅔ cup chopped fresh Italian parsley

2 sprigs fresh rosemary, chopped

2 sprigs fresh thyme, chopped

1½ teaspoons kosher salt

1½ teaspoons ground black pepper

1 teaspoon garlic powder

¼ cup plus 2 tablespoons olive oil, divided

3 cups sliced carrots

2 cups chopped celery

2 cups quartered fresh baby bella mushrooms

1 large white onion, chopped

2 (1.5-ounce) packages beef stew seasoning mix*

1 (6-ounce) can tomato paste

4 cups water

1 (32-ounce) container beef broth

2½ pounds russet potatoes, peeled and cut into 1-inch cubes

Rolls, to serve

1. Place meat in a zip-top bag; add parsley, rosemary, thyme, salt, pepper, garlic powder, and 2 tablespoons oil; seal and toss to coat.

2. In a large Dutch oven, heat remaining ¼ cup oil over medium-high heat. Working in batches, cook beef until browned on all sides, 4 to 5 minutes. Remove meat, and set aside. Drain excess fat, leaving 2 tablespoons in Dutch oven.

3. In same Dutch oven, add carrots, celery, mushrooms, onion, beef stew seasoning mix, and tomato paste, stirring to combine. Add cooked meat, 4 cups water, and broth; cover, reduce heat to medium-low, and let simmer for 1 hour and 30 minutes, stirring occasionally.

4. Stir in potatoes, cover, and cook until meat and vegetables are tender, about 1 hour and 15 minutes to 1 hour and 30 minutes more, stirring occasionally. Serve warm with rolls.

I use McCormick Classic Beef Stew Seasoning Mix.

HOT TIP: When you pick out your chuck roast, find one with a lot of white marbling. That means it will be tender and taste real good in this stew.

World's Second-Best Chili

Makes 12 to 14 servings

I would say this is the world's best chili, but my other Award-Winning Texas Chili on page 177 won first place in a statewide Texas chili cook-off, so I reckon this one is second-best. Some folks say they like this one better, though. I guess you should try both just in case.

4 pounds ground beef
2 large fresh jalapeños, chopped
1 large yellow onion, chopped
3 ounces chili seasoning*
2 tablespoons minced fresh garlic
1 (6-ounce) can tomato paste
1 (12-ounce) bottle amber Mexican beer*
1 (28-ounce) can diced tomatoes
1 (28-ounce) can tomato sauce
1 (4-ounce) can chopped green chiles (undrained)
1 tablespoon stone-ground mustard*
1 cup beef broth
2 (15.5-ounce) cans chili starter with beans*
2 tablespoons Pepper Belly Pete's Zippy-Zap Sauce
Fried pork rinds, to serve

1. In a large Dutch oven, cook ground beef over medium-high heat, stirring occasionally, until browned, 10 to 12 minutes. Drain, if necessary. Return beef to Dutch oven.

2. Stir in jalapeños, onion, chili seasoning, garlic, tomato paste, and beer, scraping up any bits on bottom of pot. Stir in diced tomatoes, tomato sauce, chiles, mustard, and broth; cover, reduce heat to medium-low, and let simmer for 2 hours, stirring occasionally.

3. Stir in chili starter and Zippy-Zap Sauce; cover and let simmer for 1 hour more. Serve hot with fried pork rinds.

I use Williams Original Chili Seasoning, Dos Equis® Ambar Especial, Inglehoffer Original Stone Ground Mustard, and Bush's Chili Magic® Campfire Style Chili Starter (medium heat) (found at Walmart).

 **HOT TIP:** Ask your butcher to coarsely grind the beef. Some folks call that chili ground. Using good-quality ground beef can make a big difference in this recipe.

Loaded Chicken and Biscuit Soup

Makes about 6 quarts

**If chicken and dumplings had a soup cousin, this would be the recipe for it.
And if you're feeling under the weather, this soup will set you right.**

½   cup unsalted butter
4   cloves garlic, minced
2   cups chopped celery
2   cups chopped carrot
2   cups chopped white onion
2   cups chopped green onion
1   tablespoon poultry seasoning
1   tablespoon ground black pepper,
     plus more to serve
1   teaspoon seasoned salt
4   (32-ounce) containers chicken
     broth
1   (22-ounce) can cream of chicken
     soup
1   tablespoon chopped fresh thyme
3   (7.5-ounce) cans buttermilk
     biscuits
½   cup all-purpose flour
1   large rotisserie chicken

1. In a large stockpot, add butter, garlic, celery, carrot, onion, and green onion. Cook over medium heat until vegetables begin to soften, about 15 to 20 minutes. Add poultry seasoning, pepper, seasoned salt, broth, and soup, stirring to combine. Continue cooking until vegetables are softened, about 10 minutes more. Add thyme.

2. Remove biscuits from cans, and flatten with palm to about 3-inch-thick disks. Cut into fourths.

3. In a medium bowl, add flour; roll biscuit pieces in flour.

4. Bring soup to a gentle boil over medium-high heat.

5. Add floured biscuits to soup, stirring constantly. Reduce heat to medium-low, cover, and let simmer for 30 minutes, stirring occasionally. While soup simmers, shred chicken, discarding skin and bones. Stir in shredded chicken, and turn off the heat. Cover and let stand for 10 minutes. Sprinkle with additional pepper, if desired. Serve immediately.

CHAPTER 5

EASY DINNERS

AFTER A LONG DAY OF WORK, IT'S NICE TO COME HOME AND PUT SOMETHING WARM ON THE TABLE FOR YOUR FAMILY. THESE RECIPES ARE GOOD ANY NIGHT OF THE WEEK.

Jambalaya

Makes about 8 servings

I don't care if you're from Cajun country or not—if you like food that tastes good, you're gonna like this one.

2½ pounds boneless, skinless chicken thighs, cut into 1-inch cubes

2 tablespoons plus 1½ teaspoons Cajun seasoning*, divided

1½ teaspoons cayenne pepper

1½ teaspoons ground black pepper

5 slices bacon, cut into 1-inch pieces

1 pound smoked andouille sausage, cut into ½-inch slices

6 cloves garlic, minced

1 large yellow onion, chopped

1 large red bell pepper, finely chopped

1 fresh jalapeño, finely chopped

1 cup chopped celery

⅓ cup unsalted butter

2 tablespoons Worcestershire sauce

3 dried bay leaves

3 cups chicken broth

1 tablespoon Pepper Belly Pete's Zippy-Zap Sauce

1 (10-ounce) can hot diced tomatoes with habaneros, puréed

2 cups long-grain rice

1. In a medium bowl, add chicken, 1½ teaspoons Cajun seasoning, cayenne pepper, and black pepper, tossing to combine. Set aside.

2. In a large Dutch oven, cook bacon over medium-high heat, stirring occasionally, until crispy, 5 to 7 minutes. Let drain on paper towels.

3. In the same Dutch oven, cook sausage over medium-high heat, stirring occasionally, until browned, about 8 minutes. Remove from pan, reserving drippings in pan, and let drain on paper towels.

4. Add garlic, onion, bell pepper, jalapeño, celery, butter, and Worcestershire; cook over medium heat, stirring occasionally, until softened, about 15 minutes.

5. Add chicken to vegetables, and cook until vegetables are tender, about 15 minutes. Stir in cooked bacon, cooked sausage, bay leaves, broth, Zippy-Zap Sauce, and remaining 2 tablespoons Cajun seasoning; bring to a gentle boil. Reduce heat to medium-low. Stir in tomatoes, and simmer for about 30 minutes. Stir in rice, cover, and cook until rice is tender, 25 to 30 minutes, stirring twice. Remove from heat and uncover; let stand for 5 to 10 minutes. Remove bay leaves just before serving. Serve hot.

*I use Cajun Two-Step.

Spaghetti and Meat Sauce

Makes about 8 to 10 servings

Don't buy that premade sauce at the grocery store when it's so easy to make at home—and it's going to taste better, too.

1½   **pounds ground sirloin**
½   **pound ground mild Italian sausage**
2   **cups diced white onion, divided**
1   **tablespoon dried Italian seasoning**
1   **tablespoon crushed red pepper**
2   **teaspoons kosher salt, divided**
1½   **teaspoons ground black pepper, divided**
1   **cup sliced baby bella mushrooms**
2   **tablespoons olive oil**
12   **fresh basil leaves, divided**
3   **cloves garlic, pressed**
2½   **pounds Campari tomatoes, halved**
½   **cup sliced celery**
¾   **pound spaghetti pasta**
French bread and grated Parmesan cheese, to serve

1. In a large Dutch oven, add ground sirloin, sausage, and 1 cup onion; cook and crumble over medium-high heat until meat is cooked through, 8 to 10 minutes. Stir in Italian seasoning, crushed red pepper, 1 teaspoon salt, and 1 teaspoon black pepper. Cook for 2 minutes. Stir in mushrooms. Remove from Dutch oven, and wipe clean.

2. In same Dutch oven, add oil, 6 basil leaves, garlic, tomatoes, celery, remaining 1 cup onion, remaining 1 teaspoon salt, and remaining ½ teaspoon black pepper. Cook over medium-low heat until tender, about 10 minutes. Remove from heat, and let cool for at least 30 minutes.

3. In the container of a blender, add tomato mixture, and pulse 4 to 5 times until chunky.

4. Add meat mixture and tomato mixture back to Dutch oven. Stir in remaining 6 basil leaves, and bring to a simmer over medium-low heat. Let simmer for 20 minutes.

5. Meanwhile, cook pasta according to package directions. Stir into sauce. Serve immediately with bread and grated Parmesan cheese.

HOT TIP: Spaghetti sauce doesn't need sugar if you buy the right tomatoes. Campari tomatoes make a big difference in the way your sauce turns out—so make sure to buy these.

WATCH MY RECIPE VIDEO HERE.

Modified Mississippi Beef Pot Roast

Makes 8 to 10 servings

My videos for this recipe have gotten more than 200 million views on social media. I can tell ya right now, folks keep watching because it delivers. Try it for yourself and see.

1	tablespoon olive oil
4	pounds boneless beef chuck roast
2	tablespoons Montreal steak seasoning
¼	cup unsalted butter
3	cups sliced carrots (about ½-inch pieces)
1	large yellow onion, chopped
1	(16-ounce) jar whole peperoncini* (undrained)
1	(1.5-ounce) package beef stew mix*
1	(1-ounce) package au jus gravy mix*
1	(1-ounce) package ranch seasoning*
1	(15-ounce) can tomato sauce
1	cup water

Hot mashed potatoes, to serve

1. In a 12-inch cast-iron skillet, heat oil over medium-high heat. Rub beef on all sides with steak seasoning. Cook meat until lightly browned, 2 to 3 minutes per side. Remove from skillet, and place in a 6-quart slow cooker.

2. In the same skillet, melt butter over medium heat. Add carrots, onion, peperoncini, stew mix, gravy mix, ranch seasoning, tomato sauce, and 1 cup water, stirring to combine. Let simmer, stirring frequently, until thickened, 5 to 6 minutes.

3. Pour vegetable mixture over steak in slow cooker. Cover and cook on high until meat is tender and shreds with a fork, about 8 hours.

4. Remove meat, and using 2 forks, shred meat. Stir meat back into slow cooker, and keep warm. Serve over mashed potatoes, if desired.

I use Mezzetta Golden Greek Peperoncini Medium Heat, McCormick® Classic Beef Stew Seasoning Mix, McCormick® Au Jus Gravy Mix, Hidden Valley® Original Ranch® Seasoning & Salad Dressing Mix.

STEP-BY-STEP

If you try one recipe in this cookbook, it oughta be this one. This is the most popular recipe video I've ever had, and it's no wonder—this recipe brings the magic every time. Go ahead and see for yourself.

1. Season your beef on all sides. Don't be shy.

2. In a cast-iron skillet, sear the meat on all sides. Use tongs, and be careful! Then, put it in the slow cooker.

3. Use the same skillet and all the other ingredients. Stir everything together and let it all simmer for a bit.

4. Pour the vegetable mixture into the slow cooker over the seared beef.

5. After about 8 hours, you can take the cooked beef out of the slow cooker. Shred the meat on a cutting board.

6. Serve it up over some mashed potatoes. And get ready—your family's gonna love this one.

I know some folks don't use slow cookers very much, but I'm not sure why. I've found using slow cookers to be one of the easiest ways to make sure you and your family get hot meals on the table at supper time. If you haven't gotten yours out in a while, get it back out and try a new recipe. You might just remember why they're so handy.

LOW AND SLOW

Just about any soup or stew, even ones with bulky potatoes and big hunks of meat, will be tender and ready for eating if you cook it on low for about 8 hours. Put your ingredients in your slow cooker before work in the morning, and you'll come home to a fully cooked meal.

GIVE IT A SEAR

Don't skip this step unless you absolutely don't have time for it. If you're cooking a big roast, I suggest searing it on all sides before putting it in your slow cooker. This will help to seal in the juices and make sure your meat doesn't dry out during the cooking process.

WORK AHEAD

If you know you're not a morning person (I can relate) and that doing any extra steps before work will cause you stress, you might want to prep your food the night before. Not everything can be done ahead, but some things, like chopping carrots or trimming the fat off meat, can be done ahead of time to make your mornings faster.

BE CHEAP

Slow cooker recipes are great for cheap cuts of meat. Whenever I see a pork shoulder, round steak, chuck roast, or other big cuts of meat for a good price, I always get them. After cooking for 8 hours in the slow cooker, they taste as good as anything you'd get at one of those fancy restaurants.

Extreme Ham and Cheese

Makes 8 to 10 servings

This recipe is like taking a simple sandwich and giving it a big upgrade. It's a quick dinner that's sure to get a round of applause from the family.

1   (16-ounce) package rotini pasta
¼   cup unsalted butter
5   slices bacon, cooked and chopped
3   fresh jalapeños, chopped
1   teaspoon garlic powder
1   teaspoon Cajun seasoning*
1   (12-ounce) can evaporated milk
1   tablespoon Pepper Belly Pete's Zippy-Zap Sauce
1   teaspoon Worcestershire sauce
1   (8-ounce) package cream cheese, cubed and softened
1   (8-ounce) package shredded Monterey Jack cheese with peppers
1   (8-ounce) block pasteurized processed cheese product*, cubed
8   ounces chopped Black Forest ham
2   cups shredded smoked mozzarella cheese

1. Preheat oven to 350°. Lightly grease an 11x7-inch baking dish with cooking spray. Cook pasta according to package directions.
2. In a large nonstick skillet, melt butter over medium heat; add bacon, jalapeños, garlic powder, Cajun seasoning, evaporated milk, Zippy-Zap Sauce, Worcestershire, cream cheese, Monterey Jack cheese, and processed cheese. Cook, stirring constantly, until cheese is melted. Stir in cooked pasta and ham. Spoon into prepared dish. Sprinkle mozzarella evenly over top.
3. Bake until cheese is melted, 15 to 20 minutes. Serve immediately.

*I use Cajun Two-Step and Velveeta® Cheese.

Shrimp Fried Rice

Makes 4 to 6 servings

Some folks get nervous about making fried rice, but it's really an easy one-pot dinner. If your family doesn't like shrimp, you can just add cooked chicken, steak, or salmon at the very end. Make it how you like it.

2   tablespoons vegetable oil
1   cup chopped white onion
1   serrano pepper, minced
1   cup frozen mixed vegetables, thawed
3   cups day-old cooked rice
2   tablespoons unsalted butter
1   tablespoon minced garlic
12   medium fresh shrimp, peeled and deveined
2   large eggs, lightly beaten
2   tablespoons soy sauce
¼   teaspoon kosher salt
1   teaspoon ground black pepper

1. In a large stainless steel skillet, heat oil over medium-high heat. Add onion to one side and serrano pepper and mixed vegetables to the other; cook, stirring each occasionally, for 1 to 2 minutes.

2. Add rice, butter, and garlic, leaving space on opposite sides of the pan. Add shrimp to one open space and eggs to the other. Add soy sauce, salt, and black pepper all over. Cook eggs, stirring constantly, until cooked through. Meanwhile, cook shrimp, turning occasionally, until pink.

3. Increase heat to high, and mix everything together until incorporated, 1 to 2 minutes. Serve hot.

Wylie and me behind the Bass Pro Shops on the Shreveport Boardwalk.

Stuffed Bell Peppers

Makes 6

This is the easiest way to make **Stuffed Bell Peppers**. They were big back in the '90s for a reason—now everybody's started making them again. What are you waiting for?

6   large orange bell peppers
1½   pounds ground beef
1   (1-ounce) package taco seasoning
1   (16-ounce) can smooth refried beans
1   teaspoon garlic powder
1   teaspoon onion powder
1   teaspoon ground cumin
1   teaspoon chili powder
1   teaspoon ground black pepper
1   cup chunky salsa*
1   (8-ounce) package cream cheese, cubed and softened
1½   cups finely shredded medium Cheddar cheese

1. Preheat oven to 350°. Lightly grease 6 wells of a 6- or 12-well muffin tin with cooking spray.

2. Cut ¼ inch off the top of each bell pepper, saving tops for other uses, and remove membranes and seeds.

3. In a large Dutch oven, add bell peppers and water to cover by ½ inch. Bring to a gentle boil over medium-high heat. Reduce heat to medium, and simmer until bell peppers are mostly tender but still hold their shape, 6 to 7 minutes. Remove, and drain well.

4. In a large nonstick skillet, cook and crumble ground beef and taco seasoning over medium-high heat until browned, 8 to 10 minutes. Stir in beans, garlic powder, onion powder, cumin, chili powder, black pepper, salsa, and cream cheese. Reduce heat to medium, and continue cooking, stirring frequently, until cream cheese is melted, 3 to 4 minutes more.

5. Place 1 bell pepper in each of the 6 prepared wells, and spoon meat mixture evenly into each. Sprinkle shredded cheese evenly on top.

6. Bake until cheese is melted and bell peppers are tender, about 20 minutes. Serve hot.

I use Pace Medium Salsa.

Slow Cooker Chicken Rigatoni

Makes about 12 servings

Cheese, chicken, and pasta in an easy one-pot meal—you can't go wrong. Even picky eaters will like this one.

4   boneless skinless chicken breasts (about 1½ pounds)
1   (1-ounce) package dried onion soup and dip mix
1   tablespoon dried Italian seasoning
1½ teaspoons garlic powder
1½ teaspoons ground black pepper
3   cups chicken broth, divided
2   cups heavy whipping cream
1   (10.5-ounce) can cream of chicken soup
2   tablespoons Pepper Belly Pete's Zippy-Zap Sauce
1   (8-ounce) package cream cheese
¼   cup unsalted butter
1   pound rigatoni pasta
2   cups shredded Parmesan cheese
2   cups shredded smoked Gouda cheese
Toppings: chopped fresh parsley, ground black pepper

1. In a 6-quart slow cooker, combine chicken, soup mix, Italian seasoning, garlic powder, pepper, 1½ cups broth, cream, soup, Zippy-Zap Sauce, cream cheese, and butter. Cover and cook on low until chicken can be shredded, 2 hours to 2 hours and 30 minutes.
2. Using 2 forks, shred chicken in the pot. Stir in pasta and Parmesan cheese. Top with Gouda and remaining 1½ cups broth. Cover and cook on low until pasta is tender, about 45 minutes. Top with parsley and pepper, if desired.

Talking on the phone. I was about 3 years old. This was taken in the house where I live now. My parents moved it to this spot in the early 1970s from a nearby town.

Mama's Salmon Patties

Makes 5 servings

My mama made Salmon Patties for dinner a lot when I was a kid. I still have her old recipe card she wrote out. It wasn't my favorite meal as a kid, but they started tasting better the older I got. Now I love them—maybe they were just missing the Zippy-Zap Sauce back then.

1   **(14.75-ounce) can pink salmon, drained**
10   **buttery round crackers*, finely crushed**
½   **cup chopped green onion**
1   **teaspoon garlic powder**
1   **teaspoon cayenne pepper**
1   **teaspoon ground black pepper**
1   **large egg**
1   **cup plus 1 tablespoon all-purpose flour, divided**
Vegetable oil, for frying
Pepper Belly Pete's Zippy-Zap Sauce and lemon slices, to serve

1. In a medium bowl, add salmon, and break into small pieces with a fork. Stir in crushed crackers, green onion, garlic powder, cayenne pepper, black pepper, and egg. Sprinkle in 1 tablespoon flour, stirring to combine.

2. Divide mixture into 5 equal parts, and shape each into a ball; flatten into patties, about ½ inch thick. Dredge each patty in remaining 1 cup flour, pressing patties to hold their shape.

3. In a medium nonstick skillet, heat ½ inch oil over medium-high heat until a deep-fry thermometer registers 350°. Working in batches, cook patties in hot oil until browned on both sides, 2 to 3 minutes per side. Serve warm with Zippy-Zap Sauce and lemon slices, if desired.

*I use Ritz crackers.

My mother's recipe box. I have it in my kitchen now and pull it down when I need some inspiration.

Vegetable Beef

Makes 8 to 10 servings

If your kids don't like vegetables, this recipe is a good way to sneak them in. A side of cornbread doesn't hurt either.

¼ cup unsalted butter
2 fresh jalapeños, chopped
1 large white onion, chopped
1 tablespoon Worcestershire sauce
1 tablespoon Pepper Belly Pete's Zippy-Zap Sauce
3 pounds ground beef
1 (6-ounce) can tomato paste
1 tablespoon dried Italian seasoning
1 tablespoon ground black pepper
2 cups half-moon-sliced carrots
2 cups frozen corn kernels, thawed
2 cups trimmed green beans
1 (15-ounce) can diced fire-roasted tomatoes
1 (15-ounce) can tomato sauce
2 tablespoons minced garlic
2 cups beef broth
Hot cooked rice, pasta, or cornbread, to serve

1. In large cast-iron skillet, melt butter over medium-high heat. Add jalapeños, onion, Worcestershire, and Zippy-Zap Sauce, and cook until tender, 2 to 3 minutes. Add beef, tomato paste, Italian seasoning, and black pepper; cook and crumble until browned, 8 to 10 minutes. Stir in carrots, corn, green beans, diced tomatoes, tomato sauce, garlic, and broth. Cover, reduce heat to medium-low, and let simmer for 1 hour. Serve hot over rice, pasta, or cornbread.

Easy Beef Stroganoff

Makes 8 to 10 servings

There's not much better than a creamy and cheesy beef stroganoff. When you put this down on the dinner table, everybody's going to be fighting about who gets the next helping.

3	pounds ground sirloin
1½	teaspoons garlic powder
1½	teaspoons ground black pepper
1	teaspoon cayenne pepper
1	(8-ounce) package sliced baby bella mushrooms
1	bunch green onion, sliced
1	(2.2-ounce) box beefy onion soup mix* (both packages)
1	(10.5-ounce) can cream of mushroom soup
1	cup half-and-half
½	cup sour cream
½	cup condensed beef broth
1	(8-ounce) package cream cheese, softened
1	(12-ounce) bag egg noodle dumplings*
¼	cup grated Parmesan cheese
1	(16-ounce) package shredded mozzarella cheese
1	teaspoon dried parsley flakes

1. Preheat oven to 350°. Lightly grease a 4-quart baking dish with cooking spray.

2. In a large Dutch oven, cook sirloin over medium-high heat, breaking up meat as it cooks. Stir in garlic powder, black pepper, and cayenne pepper. Stir in mushrooms, green onion, soup mix, soup, half-and-half, sour cream, broth, and cream cheese. Reduce heat to medium-low, and let simmer until beef and mushrooms are cooked through and onions are tender, about 10 minutes.

3. Meanwhile, cook egg noodles according to package directions. Stir cooked noodles into beef mixture.

4. Remove from heat, and spoon into prepared dish. Sprinkle with Parmesan, mozzarella, and parsley flakes.

5. Bake until cheese is melted and casserole is bubbly, about 30 minutes. Serve warm.

I use Lipton Beefy Onion Recipe Soup & Dip Mix and No Yolks Cholesterol Free Egg White Pasta Dumplings.

HOT TIP: This is a good meal to make in a disposable pan. It makes it easier to pack it up and take to your neighbor's house for your next potluck (that's assuming you want to share).

Skillet Lick Chicken

Makes 8 servings

If you know anyone who doesn't like broccoli, feed them this Skillet Lick Chicken. They'll be eating it so fast they'll blister their tongue.

2 tablespoons olive oil
3 tablespoons unsalted butter
1 medium white onion, chopped
2 tablespoons Pepper Belly Pete's Zippy-Zap Sauce
2 tablespoons minced garlic
1 tablespoon garlic powder
1 tablespoon crushed red pepper
1 tablespoon ground black pepper
4 cups shredded rotisserie chicken
4 cups orzo
3 cups broccoli florets
1 (32-ounce) container chicken stock
1 (8-ounce) block white American cheese, cubed
½ cup heavy whipping cream

1. Heat a large stainless steel skillet over medium heat. Add oil, butter, onion, and Zippy-Zap Sauce; cook until butter melts, 2 to 3 minutes. Add minced garlic, garlic powder, red pepper, and black pepper, stirring until combined. Add chicken, orzo, broccoli, chicken stock, and cheese; reduce heat to low, and bring to a gentle boil. Cook, stirring occasionally, until cheese has melted and pasta is tender, about 20 minutes. Add cream, and cook, stirring constantly, until the pasta is cooked through, 4 to 5 minutes. Serve warm.

CHAPTER 6

COMFORT
FOOD

SOME DAYS, YOU JUST WANT TO EAT
SOMETHING THAT MAKES YOU FEEL
GOOD, SOMETHING LIKE YOUR MAMA
USED TO MAKE. THESE RECIPES
WILL SET YOU RIGHT.

Sloppy Joes

Makes 6 servings

Remember sloppy joe day in the school cafeteria? Those lunch ladies knew what they were doing, but I have to say, my version might be even better.

2   tablespoons unsalted butter
1   large white onion, chopped
1   green bell pepper, chopped
2   pounds lean ground sirloin
2   tablespoons packed light brown sugar
2   teaspoons ground black pepper
1   teaspoon garlic salt
1   teaspoon smoked paprika
1   cup ketchup
1   cup tomato sauce
2   tablespoons apple cider vinegar
2   tablespoons Worcestershire sauce
2   tablespoons yellow mustard
6   sesame seed hamburger buns
3   tablespoons unsalted butter, melted
Shredded Colby-Jack cheese blend and Pepper Belly Pete's Zippy-Zap Sauce, to serve

1. In large nonstick skillet, melt butter over medium-high heat. Add onion and bell pepper, and cook, stirring frequently, until tender, 4 to 5 minutes. Add beef, and cook and crumble, stirring frequently, until browned, 6 to 8 minutes. Stir in brown sugar, black pepper, garlic salt, paprika, ketchup, tomato sauce, vinegar, Worcestershire, and mustard. Reduce heat to medium, and let simmer until desired thickness is reached, about 15 minutes.

2. Heat a griddle over medium heat. Brush cut side of all buns with melted butter. Place, cut side down, on hot griddle. Cook until golden brown, 1 to 2 minutes. Spoon ground beef mixture evenly on bottom half of buns, and top each with cheese and Zippy-Zap Sauce, if desired. Top with top half of buns, cut side down. Serve immediately.

Fried Chicken Salad

Makes about 6

It's like regular chicken salad but better. Once you fry it up this way,
you won't want it any other way.

3 cups shredded cooked chicken breast
2 cloves garlic, minced
1 medium avocado, peeled, pitted, and chopped
1 fresh jalapeño, minced
¼ cup finely chopped celery
¼ cup chopped red onion
¼ cup plus 1 tablespoon mayonnaise, divided
½ teaspoon yellow mustard
½ teaspoon Pepper Belly Pete's Zippy-Zap Sauce
2 teaspoons ground black pepper, divided
Vegetable oil, for frying
2½ cups all-purpose flour
1½ teaspoons Cajun seasoning*
3 large eggs
3 tablespoons water
Salsa, to serve

1. Line a large baking sheet with foil and grease with cooking spray.
2. In large bowl, add chicken, garlic, avocado, jalapeño, celery, onion, ¼ cup mayonnaise, mustard, Zippy-Zap Sauce, and 1 teaspoon black pepper, stirring to combine. Add remaining 1 tablespoon mayonnaise if mixture does not come together easily. Form into patties, about ½ cup each. Place on prepared baking sheet. Freeze for 30 minutes.
3. In a 12-inch cast-iron skillet, heat ½ inch oil over medium heat until a deep-fry thermometer registers 350°. Line a baking sheet with paper towels.
4. In a large bowl, whisk together flour, Cajun seasoning, and remaining 1 teaspoon black pepper.
5. In a medium bowl, whisk together eggs and 3 tablespoons water.
6. Dip 1 patty in flour mixture, shaking off excess, and dip in egg mixture. Place back in flour mixture, and coat well, shaking off excess. Repeat with remaining patties.
7. Working in batches, fry patties until browned on both sides, 3 to 5 minutes per side. Let drain on prepared pan. Serve warm with salsa.

*I use Cajun Two-Step.

Best Beef Tips Ever

Makes 6 to 8 servings

From age 5 to 105, everybody's gonna love these beef tips served over mashed potatoes. It's the king of comfort food.

2½ pounds boneless beef short ribs, cut into 1½-inch cubes
2   teaspoons Montreal steak seasoning
2   tablespoons vegetable oil
2   cups chopped white onion
1   (8-ounce) package sliced baby bella mushrooms
½   cup dry red wine
2   tablespoons Worcestershire sauce
2   tablespoons soy sauce
2   tablespoons dill pickle juice
2   tablespoons Pepper Belly Pete's Zippy-Zap Sauce
2   tablespoons minced garlic
1   (1.5-ounce) package beef stew mix
1   (0.87-ounce) package brown gravy mix
1   tablespoon ground black pepper
2   cups warm water (103°)
Mashed potatoes and ground black pepper, to serve

1. In a medium bowl, toss beef with steak seasoning until coated.

2. In a large cast-iron skillet, heat oil over medium-high heat. Add seasoned beef in batches, and cook until browned, 5 to 7 minutes per batch. Remove from skillet with a slotted spoon.

3. In the same skillet, add onion, mushrooms, red wine, Worcestershire, soy sauce, pickle juice, and Zippy-Zap Sauce, stirring constantly to prevent it from sticking to the bottom of the pan. Add garlic, beef stew mix, brown gravy mix, pepper, and 2 cups warm water; mix well. Bring to a gentle boil, stirring constantly; remove from heat.

4. In a slow cooker, add meat and gravy mixture; cover and cook on low heat until beef is tender, 4 to 5 hours.

5. Spread beef tips and gravy over mashed potatoes. Sprinkle with pepper. Serve immediately.

Fish and Chips

Makes 6 servings

Some folks might think fish and chips is just for the Brits, but it tastes pretty good in Texas (and anywhere else, for that matter).

2½ pounds Yukon gold potatoes, cut into ¼-inch-thick slices
Vegetable oil, for frying
4 cups all-purpose flour, divided
4 cups rice flour, divided
2 (12-ounce) bottles Mexican amber beer
1 (1.7-ounce) bottle vodka
1 teaspoon Pepper Belly Pete's Zippy-Zap Sauce, plus more to serve
2 teaspoons ground black pepper, divided, plus more to taste
6 cod fish fillets (about 6 ounces each)
1½ teaspoons kosher salt, plus more to taste
1½ teaspoons smoked paprika
Sea salt flakes, for sprinkling
Tartar sauce, to serve

1. In a large stockpot, add potatoes and water to cover by 1 inch, and bring to a gentle boil over medium-high heat. Reduce heat to medium-low, and let simmer until potatoes are mostly tender but still hold their shape, 7 to 9 minutes. Drain well, and pat dry with paper towels. Let cool completely.
2. In a large Dutch oven, fill halfway with oil. Heat oil over medium-high heat until a deep-fry thermometer registers 350°. Line 2 baking sheets with paper towels.
3. In a large bowl, sift together 2 cups all-purpose flour and 2 cups rice flour.
4. In a separate large bowl, sift together remaining 2 cups all-purpose flour and remaining 2 cups rice flour. Whisk in beer, vodka, Zippy-Zap Sauce, and ½ teaspoon pepper.
5. Season fish evenly with kosher salt, paprika, and remaining 1½ teaspoons pepper. Dredge each fish fillet in dry flour mixture, shaking off any extra. Then dip in beer mixture, letting excess drip off.
6. Working in batches, fry fish until golden brown on both sides and an internal temperature of 145° is reached, 6 to 8 minutes, turning occasionally. Remove with a slotted spoon, and let drain on paper towels. Sprinkle with sea salt. (To keep fish warm after frying, place on a baking sheet lined with parchment paper. Place baking sheet in oven preheated to 200° until serving.)
7. Heat oil over medium heat until a deep-fry thermometer registers 320°. Working in batches, fry potatoes until soft but not browned, 2 to 3 minutes. Remove from oil using a slotted spoon; let drain on one prepared pan.
8. Increase heat to high, and heat oil until a deep-fry thermometer registers 375°. Working in batches, fry potatoes until golden brown, 3 to 5 minutes more. Remove from oil using a slotted spoon, and let drain on remaining prepared pan. While hot, sprinkle with sea salt and pepper to taste. Serve hot with fried potatoes and tartar sauce.

King Ranch Chicken

Makes 8 servings

I always love a great-tasting casserole that will feed a lot of people. This recipe is one to mark because you're gonna keep coming back to it.

1   **tablespoon unsalted butter**
3   **cloves garlic, minced**
1   **medium white onion, diced**
1   **fresh jalapeño, diced**
1   **cube tomato bouillon with chicken flavor**
1   **teaspoon garlic powder**
1   **teaspoon chili powder**
1   **teaspoon ground black pepper**
1   **(10-ounce) can diced tomatoes with green chiles**
1   **cup chicken broth**
1   **(10.5-ounce) can cream of chicken soup**
1   **(10.5-ounce) can cream of mushroom soup**
1   **(10-ounce) container queso quesadilla cheese**
5   **cups shredded rotisserie chicken**
16   **corn tortillas, divided**
1½   **cups shredded Colby-Jack cheese blend**

1. Preheat oven to 350°. Lightly grease a 13x9-inch baking dish with cooking spray.

2. In a large saucepan, melt butter over medium heat. Add garlic, onion, jalapeño, and bouillon; cook until onions have softened and garlic is fragrant, 4 to 5 minutes. Add garlic powder, chili powder, and black pepper, stirring to combine, and cook until fragrant, about 1 minute. Add tomatoes and chicken broth, stirring to combine; cook until mixture begins to gently boil, 4 to 5 minutes. Add soups and queso cheese; mix together and let simmer, stirring constantly, until cheese melts, 3 to 4 minutes. Stir in chicken; remove from heat.

3. Arrange 8 tortillas in bottom of prepared dish. Spread half of the chicken mixture onto tortillas; layer remaining 8 tortillas on top, and then spread the remaining chicken mixture on top. Top with Colby-Jack cheese.

4. Cover with foil, and bake until cheese has melted, 20 to 25 minutes. Remove foil, and let bake until cheese has slightly browned, about 5 minutes more. Let cool slightly before serving.

Beef Thit Kho

Makes 6 to 8 servings

A Vietnamese man I worked with back in the '90s shared this recipe with me.
He made it with pork, but I really like it with beef. These ribs end up
fall-apart tender, and the egg absorbs all the flavor—that's a win-win.

2 pounds boneless beef short ribs, trimmed and cut into 1-inch cubes
1 teaspoon kosher salt
1 teaspoon ground black pepper
½ teaspoon granulated sugar
2 tablespoons Pepper Belly Pete's Flavor-Time Sizzling Steak Sauce
⅓ cup lard or oil
2 fresh habanero peppers, seeded and sliced
1 medium white onion, chopped
5 cloves garlic, minced
1 (11.8-ounce) can coconut water
¼ cup browning seasoning*
1 teaspoon fish sauce
8 large hard-boiled eggs, peeled
1 bunch green onions, sliced
2 tablespoons balsamic vinegar
2 (3-ounce) packages ramen noodles
Pepper Belly Pete's Zippy-Zap Sauce and sliced green onion, to serve

1. In a large bowl, combine short ribs, salt, black pepper, sugar, and Sizzling Steak Sauce. Cover and let marinate at room temperature about 30 minutes.

2. In a large nonstick skillet, heat lard or oil over medium-high heat, and cook beef in 2 batches until seared on all sides, 4 to 5 minutes total. Remove meat, and set aside. Drain oil, reserving 1 tablespoon in pan.

3. In same skillet over medium-high heat, add habanero peppers and onion, and cook, stirring frequently, until softened, about 3 minutes. Add cooked meat, garlic, coconut water, browning seasoning, and fish sauce; reduce heat to medium-low, cover, and let simmer for 1 hour.

4. Take a wooden pick and pierce eggs all over. Place eggs in beef mixture, making sure you have enough liquid to submerge eggs. (Add water until the eggs are completely submerged, if needed.) Stir in green onion and vinegar; cover and cook for 45 minutes.

5. Add noodles (without seasoning packets), and cook until tender, 6 to 7 minutes. Serve immediately with Zippy-Zap Sauce and green onion, if desired.

*I use Maggi Liquid Seasoning.

HOT TIP: You can substitute 2 tablespoons of Worcestershire sauce and 2 tablespoons of soy sauce for the browning seasoning.

Pig in the Mud

Makes 4 to 6 servings

Some folks say this dish is the best thing I make. Your friends and family might say the same thing about you once you start making it. Sounds like you ought to give it a try.

2	pounds cubed country-style ribs
½	teaspoon kosher salt
½	teaspoon ground black pepper
2	tablespoons olive oil
⅓	cup low-sodium soy sauce
1	(12-ounce) cola beverage*
2	tablespoons Worcestershire sauce
1½	teaspoons red pepper flakes
1	teaspoon grated fresh ginger
2	cups sliced carrot
2	cups chopped white onion
1½	cups chopped celery
1	tablespoon cornstarch
2	tablespoons water
1	cup sliced green onion
1	tablespoon Sriracha sauce

Hot cooked rice and Pepper Belly Pete's Zippy-Zap Sauce, to serve

1. In a medium bowl, toss together ribs, salt, and pepper. Cover and let marinate for about 30 minutes in the refrigerator.

2. In a large Dutch oven, heat oil over medium-high heat. Add pork in a single layer, and cook until browned, about 4 to 5 minutes per side.

3. Add soy sauce, cola, Worcestershire, red pepper flakes, and ginger; stir together. Cover and let cook on low heat for 1 hour.

4. Uncover and skim off fat, if necessary. Stir in carrot, onion, and celery; cover and cook on low for 1 hour.

5. In a small bowl, whisk together cornstarch and 2 tablespoons water until smooth. Stir into Dutch oven until well combined. Stir in green onion. Let simmer, uncovered, for 30 minutes, stirring occasionally. Stir in Sriracha sauce. Serve over hot cooked rice with Zippy-Zap Sauce, if desired.

I use Pepsi.

My birthday party when I was turning 13. Growing up, I was a Cowboys fan. My aunt in Dallas would take us to the home games, and we always had a good time.

Unbelievable Chicken Casserole

Makes about 8 servings

I sometimes call this my **Chuck Norris** casserole because it's so good, you're not gonna to know what to think. It's going to karate chop your taste buds (in a good way).

½   **cup unsalted butter**
3   **cloves garlic, minced**
2   **cups chopped white onion**
1   **cup chopped celery**
1   **tablespoon Worcestershire sauce**
1   **teaspoon cayenne pepper**
1   **teaspoon Cajun seasoning***
1   **teaspoon ground black pepper**
1   **(8-ounce) package sliced baby bella mushrooms**
2   **cups half-and-half**
1   **(8-ounce) package cream cheese, softened**
½   **cup sour cream**
1   **(16-ounce) block Colby-Jack cheese blend, shredded**
1   **tablespoon Pepper Belly Pete's Zippy-Zap Sauce, plus more to serve**
4   **cups shredded rotisserie chicken**
1   **pound penne pasta, cooked according to package directions**
2   **cups shredded part-skim mozzarella cheese**
1   **cup finely crushed Parmesan-flavored baked cheese crackers***
2   **cups shredded sharp Cheddar cheese**

1. Preheat oven to 350°. Lightly grease a 13x9-inch baking dish with tall sides with cooking spray.

2. In a large Dutch oven, melt butter over medium-high heat. Add garlic, onion, celery, Worcestershire, cayenne pepper, Cajun seasoning, and black pepper. Cook, stirring constantly, until vegetables are tender, about 5 minutes. Stir in mushrooms, half-and-half, cream cheese, sour cream, Colby-Jack cheese, and Zippy-Zap Sauce. Reduce heat to medium, and let simmer until cheese is melted, stirring frequently, about 5 minutes. Stir in chicken and pasta. Remove from heat, and stir until incorporated.

3. Spoon half of pasta mixture into prepared pan. Sprinkle mozzarella cheese evenly over pasta mixture. Spoon the remaining pasta mixture on top. Sprinkle evenly with cracker crumbs. Sprinkle evenly with Cheddar cheese.

4. Bake until bubbly and cheese is golden brown, about 30 minutes. Serve hot.

I use Cajun Two-Step and Pepperidge Farm Goldfish Parmesan Cracker.

Bacon Bourbon Meatloaf

Makes about 8 servings

This meatloaf is so good that your friends will have it all shoved in their pockets trying to take the leftovers home.

5   cloves garlic, coarsely chopped
2   fresh jalapeños, cut in half
1   large white onion, quartered
1   plum tomato, chopped
1   (4-ounce) can diced mild or hot green chiles*
3   pounds ground sirloin
1½   teaspoons ground black pepper
2   sleeves of everything-flavored buttery round crackers*, crushed
1   (8-ounce) package shredded sharp Cheddar cheese
1   cup Pepper Belly Pete's Bacon Bourbon Barbecue Sauce

1. Preheat oven to 350°. Lightly grease a 13x9-inch baking dish with cooking spray.

2. In the work bowl of a food processor, add garlic, jalapeños, onion, tomato, and green chiles; pulse until smooth.

3. In a large bowl, combine sirloin and black pepper. Add the onion mixture, crackers, and cheese; mix together with hands. Pack the mixture evenly into prepared pan.

4. Bake until golden brown, about 1 hour. Top with Bacon Bourbon Barbecue Sauce. Return to oven, and bake until caramelized or until internal temperature registers 165°, 15 to 20 minutes more. Let stand for 10 minutes before serving.

I use Hatch Green Chiles and Ritz Everything Crackers.

Stuffed Chicken

Makes 4 servings

I sometimes call this one Pig in the Chicken, but it's also a Texas version of schnitzel. Whether you eat it after skiing down the Alps or coming in after a day on the ranch, it's gonna taste good.

4   boneless skinless chicken breasts (about 10 ounces each)
1   teaspoon seasoned salt*
8   (1-ounce) slices deli smoked ham
12   (1-ounce) slices deli Swiss cheese
Vegetable oil, for frying
2   cups whole buttermilk
2   tablespoons Pepper Belly Pete's Zippy-Zap Sauce
2   cups all-purpose flour
1½   teaspoons kosher salt, divided
1½   teaspoons ground black pepper, divided
¾   teaspoon cayenne pepper, divided
2   cups panko (Japanese bread crumbs)

1. Split each chicken breast lengthwise (but do not cut all the way through) and place each in a zip-top bag. Using a meat mallet or rolling pin, flatten breasts to ¼ inch thick.

2. Open each breast and lay flat, cut side up, and sprinkle with seasoned salt. Place 2 slices ham and 3 slices cheese on each breast. Roll up long ways. Trim any excess ham and cheese, and wrap tightly with plastic wrap. Freeze for 30 minutes.

3. In a large Dutch oven, fill halfway with oil. Heat oil over medium-high heat until a deep-fry thermometer registers 350°. Line a baking sheet with paper towels.

4. In a medium bowl, whisk together buttermilk and Zippy-Zap Sauce.

5. In another medium bowl, mix together flour, 1 teaspoon kosher salt, 1 teaspoon black pepper, and ½ teaspoon cayenne pepper.

6. In another medium bowl, mix together bread crumbs, remaining ½ teaspoon kosher salt, remaining ½ teaspoon black pepper, and remaining ¼ teaspoon cayenne pepper.

7. Remove chicken from freezer. Discard plastic wrap. Dip each chicken roll in buttermilk mixture, letting extra drip off. Dredge each chicken roll in flour mixture, shaking off any extra. Place back in buttermilk mixture, letting extra drip off, and dredge in bread crumbs.

8. Working in batches, fry chicken until temperature registers 165°, 6 to 8 minutes, turning occasionally. Remove with a slotted spoon, and let drain on prepared pan. Serve warm.

*I use Lawry's Seasoned Salt.

Pig in a Pot

Makes about 8 servings

Get this slow cooker dinner going before work, and you'll come home to a great-smelling (and great-tasting) dinner waiting on you.

4   pounds boneless pork roast
1   teaspoon Cajun seasoning*, divided
½   teaspoon kosher salt
½   teaspoon ground black pepper
2   tablespoons vegetable oil
5   carrots, sliced
4   stalks celery, chopped
1   large white onion, chopped
2   tablespoons Worcestershire sauce
2   tablespoons Pepper Belly Pete's Zippy-Zap Sauce
1   (1-ounce) package au jus gravy mix
1   (0.87-ounce) package brown gravy mix
1   (1-ounce) package ranch dressing mix
1   (22-ounce) can cream of mushroom soup
1   (14.5-ounce) can beef broth
1   pound baby Yukon gold potatoes, halved

1. Butterfly pork roast. Season all over with ½ teaspoon Cajun seasoning, salt, and pepper.

2. In a 12-inch cast-iron skillet, heat oil over medium-high heat. Add roast, and cook until brown on all sides, about 4 minutes per side. Place roast in a 6-quart slow cooker.

3. In the same skillet, add carrots, celery, onion, Worcestershire, Zippy-Zap Sauce, gravy mixes, ranch seasoning, soup, and beef broth; cook over medium-low heat until bubbly and thickened, about 3 minutes. Pour gravy over pork. Top with potatoes and remaining ½ teaspoon Cajun seasoning.

4. Cover with lid, and cook on low until pork and vegetables are tender, about 8 hours. Shred pork with 2 forks. Serve warm.

I use Cajun Two-Step.

Chili Pie

Makes 8 to 10 servings

You ain't never seen comfort food like this. This will warm you up from the inside out.

1 pound ground sirloin
1 pound ground sausage
4 cloves garlic, chopped
1 medium white onion, chopped
1 fresh jalapeño, chopped
1 tablespoon chili powder
1 tablespoon ground black pepper
1 teaspoon ground cumin
1 teaspoon cayenne pepper
1 (15-ounce) can pinto beans
1 (10-ounce) can fire-roasted diced tomatoes with green chiles
2 (6.5-ounce) packages yellow cornbread mix
1½ pounds frozen Tater Tots, thawed
1 (8-ounce) package shredded Monterey Jack cheese

1. Preheat oven 375°.

2. In a 12-inch cast-iron skillet, cook sirloin and sausage over medium-high heat, stirring frequently, until cooked and crumbled, 8 to 10 minutes. Add garlic, onion, jalapeño, chili powder, black pepper, cumin, and cayenne pepper; cook, stirring constantly, until vegetables begin to become tender, 3 to 4 minutes. Stir in beans and tomatoes, and reduce heat to low.

3. Mix cornbread according to package directions (should make about 2½ cups), and evenly pour over meat mixture. Using a fork, evenly poke into top of pie, rotating fork slightly with each poke, allowing cornbread mixture to fall to the bottom and evenly distribute. Do not stir. Remove from heat, and top with Tater Tots, making a circle starting on the outside edge of the skillet to the center.

4. Bake until Tater Tots are crispy, about 30 minutes. Sprinkle evenly with cheese. Continue to bake until cheese has melted and slightly browned on edges, about 10 minutes more. Serve warm.

 **HOT TIP:** You can use whatever kind of meat you like in this recipe. I use a beef and pork blend, but you could use all beef or sub in some venison. The same goes for the beans and cheese—use what you've already got at home or what your family likes best.

Pork Chop Casserole

Makes 6 servings

Next time you get the call that your in-laws are coming over, throw this one in the oven. It doesn't take long to put together and feeds a lot of people.

4   cloves garlic, chopped
3   cups sliced carrot
3   cups quartered fresh baby bella mushrooms
2½   pounds medium Yukon gold potatoes, quartered
1   large white onion, chopped
1   large fresh jalapeño, chopped
1   cup chopped celery
1½   teaspoons ground black pepper
6   (1-inch-thick) bone-in pork chops (about 3¾ pounds each)
1½   teaspoons Cajun seasoning*
1   (1-ounce) package dried onion soup and dip mix
1   (1-ounce) package au jus gravy mix
1   (0.87-ounce) package brown gravy mix
1   (22-ounce) can cream of mushroom soup
1¾   cups vegetable broth
2   tablespoons Pepper Belly Pete's Zippy-Zap Sauce

1. Preheat oven to 350°.
2. In a 15x11-inch disposable roasting pan, add garlic, carrot, mushrooms, potatoes, onion, jalapeño, celery, and black pepper. Place pork chops on vegetables, and sprinkle Cajun seasoning evenly on both sides of pork chops.
3. In a medium bowl, whisk together soup mix, gravy mixes, soup, and broth. Pour mixture over pork chops and vegetables. Drizzle with Zippy-Zap Sauce. Cover tightly with foil.
4. Bake until pork chops and vegetables are tender, 2 hours and 45 minutes to 3 hours. Serve warm.

I use Cajun Two-Step.

Smothered Steak
in Brown Gravy

Makes 8 servings

WATCH MY RECIPE
VIDEO HERE.

Smothered and covered—it don't get much better than that! Get you a forkful of meat, gravy, and mashed potatoes. You'll think you've died and gone to heaven.

6	cups whole buttermilk
2	tablespoons Pepper Belly Pete's Flavor-Time Sizzling Steak Sauce
8	pieces cubed round steak (1½ pounds)
4	cups all-purpose flour
1	tablespoon ground black pepper
1	teaspoon kosher salt
1	teaspoon garlic powder
1	teaspoon onion powder
1	teaspoon cayenne pepper
10	slices bacon
1	medium yellow onion, chopped
2	cups sliced fresh baby bella mushrooms
2	tablespoons cornstarch
3	cups beef broth

Hot mashed potatoes, to serve

1. In a large bowl, whisk together buttermilk and Sizzling Steak Sauce until incorporated. Add steaks. Cover and let marinate in the refrigerator for 30 minutes.

2. In a large bowl, mix together flour, black pepper, salt, garlic powder, onion powder, and cayenne pepper.

3. In a large cast-iron skillet, cook bacon over medium-high heat until crisp, 8 to 10 minutes. Let drain on paper towels, reserving drippings in pan.

4. Remove each steak from buttermilk, letting any extra drip off. Dredge each steak in flour mixture, shaking off extra.

5. Working in batches, cook steak in hot bacon grease over medium-high heat until lightly golden brown (not cooking them through at this point), 3 to 4 minutes per side. Remove from heat, reserving liquid in pan, and let drain on paper towels.

6. Using the same skillet, reduce heat to medium-low. Sprinkle ¼ cup flour mixture, stirring until well combined. Add onion, and cook, stirring constantly, until softened, 3 to 4 minutes. Stir in mushrooms. Place cooked steak over onion mixture.

7. In a medium bowl, whisk together cornstarch and beef broth. Pour over steak mixture. Reduce heat to low, cover, and let simmer until tender, about 30 minutes. Serve immediately over mashed potatoes.

CHAPTER 7

COWBOY
CLASSICS

THEY SAY EVERYTHING'S BIGGER IN TEXAS, AND THAT INCLUDES THE FLAVOR. WHETHER YOU LIVE ON A CATTLE RANCH NEAR THE BORDER OR NOT, I THINK YOU'RE GONNA LIKE THESE RECIPES.

Birria Tacos

Makes 16

This recipe takes a little time, but trust me, it's worth it. These might be the best tacos you've ever had.

7   large cloves garlic
5   dried guajillo peppers, stemmed
3   dried ancho chiles, stemmed and seeded
3   fresh serrano peppers, stemmed
2   plum tomatoes, coarsely chopped
1   large yellow onion, cut into 8 wedges
1   (4-ounce) can chipotle peppers in adobo sauce
2½ teaspoons fine sea salt, divided
2½ teaspoons ground black pepper, divided
1½ teaspoons smoked paprika
½   teaspoon ground cumin
½   teaspoon dried Mexican oregano
1   (32-ounce) container beef broth
3   pounds boneless beef chuck roast, cut into 2-inch pieces
1   pound ox tails
3   tablespoons olive oil
2   cups chopped yellow onion
1   cup water
4   dried bay leaves
16   (5-inch) yellow corn tortillas
1½ cups shredded quesadilla cheese
1   cup chopped fresh cilantro
Lime wedges, to serve

1. In a large Dutch oven, stir together garlic, guajillo peppers, ancho chiles, serrano peppers, tomatoes, onion wedges, chipotle peppers, ½ teaspoon salt, ½ teaspoon black pepper, paprika, cumin, oregano, and broth. Cover and bring to a boil over high heat.

2. Reduce heat to medium-low, and let simmer, stirring occasionally, until vegetables are tender, 30 to 45 minutes. Remove from heat, uncover, and let cool for at least 30 minutes.

3. In the container of a blender, add vegetable mixture, and process until smooth.

4. In a medium bowl, add beef and ox tails. Sprinkle with remaining 2 teaspoons salt and remaining 2 teaspoons black pepper, tossing to coat.

5. In a large cast-iron skillet, heat oil over medium-high heat. Working in batches, cook meat mixture until brown, about 2 to 3 minutes per side. Place in a 6-quart slow cooker.

6. Add blended sauce, chopped onion, and 1 cup water to slow cooker, stirring to coat. Cook, uncovered, on high until it comes to a gentle boil, 30 to 45 minutes. Stir in bay leaves, cover with lid, and cook until meat can easily be shredded, about 4 hours.

7. In a small bowl, skim any oil from top of liquid in slow cooker and set aside. Remove bay leaves and discard.

8. Remove meat from slow cooker, and shred using 2 forks, discarding bones. Add meat back to slow cooker, and keep warm.

9. Heat a nonstick griddle or skillet over medium heat. Dip 1 tortilla in reserved slow cooker oil, and place on heated griddle. Add about ¼ cup shredded meat on one side of tortilla, and top with about 1 tablespoon cheese and about 1 tablespoon cilantro; fold over in half, and let cook until browned and cheese is melted, about 1 to 2 minutes per side. Repeat with remaining tortillas, remaining meat, remaining cheese, and remaining cilantro. Serve immediately with lime wedges, if desired.

Cowboy Casserole

Makes 8 to 10 servings

This one takes me way back. It's from a cookbook I made for my mom on Mother's Day back when I was in kindergarten in 1981.

2 pounds ground beef
1 medium white onion, chopped
1 (10-ounce) can hot diced tomatoes with green chiles, drained
1 (4-ounce) can diced green chiles
2 teaspoons minced garlic
1 teaspoon Worcestershire sauce
1 (1-ounce) package taco seasoning
1 tablespoon ground black pepper
1 (15-ounce) can Ranch Style Beans
2 (6-ounce) packages white cornbread mix*
1 (14.75-ounce) can cream-style corn
1 (8-ounce) package shredded Colby-Jack cheese blend
Topping: shredded Colby-Jack cheese blend

1. Preheat oven to 350°. Lightly grease a 13x9-inch baking dish with cooking spray.
2. In a 12-inch nonstick skillet, cook and crumble ground beef over medium-high heat, stirring frequently, until browned, 8 to 10 minutes. Drain and set aside.
3. In same skillet, add onion, tomatoes, chiles, garlic, and Worcestershire; cook, stirring frequently, until vegetables begin to become tender, 3 to 4 minutes. Stir in ground beef, taco seasoning, and black pepper; cook until onions are tender, 3 to 4 minutes more. Stir in beans. Remove from heat.
4. Prepare cornbread according to package directions; stir in cream-style corn and cheese.
5. Spoon meat mixture evenly into prepared pan. Pour cornbread mixture over meat mixture.
6. Bake until golden brown and a wooden pick inserted in the center comes out clean, 1 hour to 1 hour and 10 minutes. Top with shredded cheese, if desired.

I use Martha White Cornbread Mix.

Cowboy Caviar Poppers

Makes 24

If you've had cowboy caviar dip before, this takes it up a notch. I like to use the cowboy caviar mixture as a filling for bacon-wrapped poppers that can be dipped in Zippy-Zap Sauce. I bet you're gonna like them, too.

1   large head green cabbage (2½ pounds)
1   (15-ounce) can whole kernel yellow corn, drained
1   (15-ounce) can black beans, drained
1   (15-ounce) can seasoned slab bacon black-eyed peas*, drained
½   cup diced white onion
½   cup diced fresh jalapeño
1½   cups shredded mild Cheddar cheese
½   cup Italian salad dressing*
1   teaspoon Pepper Belly Pete's Zippy-Zap Sauce, plus more to serve
24   slices bacon

1. Preheat oven to 400°. Grease a wire baking rack with cooking spray and place on a foil-lined rimmed baking sheet.
2. Cut bottom core away from cabbage, and place cabbage in a large stockpot. Add water to cover by 1 inch.

Bring to a boil, and cook until slightly softened, about 10 minutes. (Cabbage leaves should peel away without tearing.) Remove leaves, and cut away hard part of the stems (about 24 leaves). Set aside.
3. In a large bowl, add corn, black beans, black-eyed peas, onion, jalapeño, cheese, salad dressing, and Zippy-Zap Sauce, stirring to combine.
4. On a cutting board, lay one cabbage leaf flat, and place 2 to 3 tablespoons (depending on size of cabbage leaf) cowboy caviar mixture on stem end. Roll up like a burrito, tucking ends of cabbage in while rolling. Take 1 slice bacon and tightly wrap around the full length of the cabbage roll, tucking the ends in; place, seam side down, onto wire rack on prepared pan. Repeat with remaining cabbage, remaining cowboy caviar mixture, and remaining bacon.
5. Bake until bacon is crisp, 30 to 35 minutes. Serve warm with Zippy-Zap Sauce, if desired.

I use Trappy's Black Eye Peas with Slab Bacon and Wish-Bone Italian Dressing.

HOT TIP: If you've got a favorite seasoning or rub, you can sprinkle some on the outside of the poppers before cooking. You can also grill these or put them on your smoker to get that charred flavor.

Green Chile Chicken and Rice

Makes about 8 servings

I believe this is one of the best recipes I've got. It's like a marriage between enchiladas and lasagna. Your family is gonna eat this up.

5   **Hatch or Anaheim green chiles**
1   **bunch fresh cilantro**
1   **cup water**
1   **tablespoon vegetable oil**
4   **cloves garlic, minced**
1   **large white onion, chopped**
2   **tablespoons unsalted butter**
1   **tablespoon Worcestershire sauce**
1   **tablespoon Pepper Belly Pete's Zippy-Zap Sauce**
1   **tablespoon tomato bouillon with chicken flavor**
1   **tablespoon ground black pepper**
1   **teaspoon ground cumin**
2   **cups heavy whipping cream**
4   **cups shredded rotisserie chicken**
12   **yellow corn tortillas, divided**
4   **cups hot cooked long-grain rice, divided**
4   **cups shredded Monterey Jack cheese, divided**

1. Preheat oven to 475°. Place chiles on a baking sheet.
2. Bake until chiles are soft and skins are charred, 8 to 10 minutes. Place chiles in a gallon-size resealable bag, seal, and let stand for 10 minutes.

When chiles are cool enough to handle, remove skins and seeds and discard.
3. In the container of a blender, add chiles, cilantro, and 1 cup water, and process until smooth.
4. Reduce oven to 350°. Lightly grease a 13x9-inch baking dish with cooking spray.
5. In a 12-inch cast-iron skillet, heat oil over medium-high heat. Add garlic, onion, butter, Worcestershire, and Zippy-Zap Sauce; cook, stirring frequently, until browned, 6 to 8 minutes. Stir in bouillon, black pepper, cumin, and cream. Reduce heat to low, and slowly stir in chile purée; cook, stirring constantly, until thickened, 8 to 10 minutes. Reserve 1¼ cups sauce, and add chicken to the remaining sauce in pan. Stir until coated and heated through.
6. In the bottom of the prepared dish, pour about ¼ cup reserved sauce, spreading to coat bottom of pan. Add 6 tortillas to line bottom of pan. Spread 2 cups rice over corn tortillas. Drizzle with ½ cup reserved sauce. Top with half of chicken mixture. Top with 2 cups cheese. Repeat layers again with remaining ingredients.
7. Bake until golden brown, 30 to 40 minutes. Serve immediately.

HOT TIP: The chiles can be grilled instead. Just preheat your grill to 475° and put the chiles directly on the grill rack. Grill them until they're soft and skins are charred, about 8 to 10 minutes.

Big Ole Porterhouse

Makes about 6 servings

Next time you see a big porterhouse on sale, get it and try this recipe. You'll be eating on this steak for a while, and you won't be sorry about that.

1	**porterhouse steak (about 3 pounds, about 2½ inches thick)**
¼	**cup Pepper Belly Pete's Flavor-Time Sizzling Steak Sauce**
1	**teaspoon kosher salt**
1	**teaspoon ground black pepper**
2	**tablespoons vegetable oil**
1	**cup unsalted butter**
12	**cloves garlic**
10	**sprigs fresh thyme**
8	**sprigs fresh rosemary**

Topping: fresh rosemary

1. Preheat oven to 350°.

2. Rub steak on all sides with Sizzling Steak Sauce and season with salt and pepper.

3. In a 12-inch cast-iron skillet, heat oil over medium-high heat, and sear steak until dark brown, 3 to 4 minutes per side.

4. Add butter, and cook until melted. Add garlic, thyme, and rosemary, and cook for about 2 minutes more, basting top of steak occasionally.

5. Place skillet in oven, and bake for 30 minutes for medium doneness. Remove from oven, and let rest on a cutting board for 20 minutes. Top with fresh rosemary, if desired.

HOT TIP: Use the leftover garlic butter on toasted bread or a baked potato to go with your steak. You're gonna feel like you're eating at a steakhouse tonight.

Award-Winning Texas Chili

Makes 12 to 16 servings

WATCH MY RECIPE VIDEO HERE.

This recipe won first place in a state of Texas chili cook-off. That's why I laugh everytime I hear someone say, "Beans don't belong in chili." My ribbon says different.

3   **pounds ground chuck**
1   **pound ground breakfast sausage**
5   **cloves garlic, chopped**
3   **fresh jalapeños, chopped**
1   **large white onion, chopped**
1   **(28-ounce) can diced tomatoes**
1   **(14.5-ounce) can diced tomatoes**
1   **(28-ounce) can tomato sauce**
1   **(15-ounce) can tomato sauce**
1   **(6-ounce) can tomato paste**
1   **(4-ounce) can diced green chiles (undrained)**
3   **(1-ounce) packages chili seasoning***
3   **(15.5-ounce) cans chili starter with beans***
Corn chips* and shredded Colby-Jack cheese blend, to serve

1. In a large stockpot, cook and crumble ground chuck over medium-high heat, stirring frequently, until browned, 8 to 10 minutes; drain and return to pot. Add sausage, garlic, jalapeños, and onion; cook, stirring frequently, until browned and crumbled, 4 to 5 minutes. Do not drain.

2. Stir in tomatoes, tomato sauce, tomato paste, chiles, and chili seasoning. Reduce heat to medium-low, cover, and simmer to infuse all flavors, stirring occasionally, for about 1 hour.

3. Stir in chili starter, and let simmer for 30 minutes, stirring occasionally. Serve hot with corn chips and cheese, if desired.

I use Williams Original Chili Seasoning, Bush's Chili Magic® Campfire Style Chili Starter (medium heat), and Fritos® Corn Chips.

Me and my dad when I was dressing up for Halloween or something. I'm not sure where that cigar came from—there's no telling!

Boudin Egg Rolls

Makes 8

This is my hands-down favorite appetizer recipe of all time. There's not much that can beat a good Cajun boudin.

Vegetable oil, for frying
8   refrigerated egg roll wrappers
8   slices Havarti cheese
2   cups crumbled boudin sausage, casings removed
½   cup cooked and crumbled thick-cut bacon
1   large egg yolk, beaten
½   cup yellow mustard
2   tablespoons Pepper Belly Pete's Zippy-Zap Sauce

1. In a large cast-iron Dutch oven, fill halfway with oil. Heat over medium-high heat until a deep-fry thermometer registers 350°. Line a baking sheet with paper towels.
2. Place 1 square egg roll wrapper on a flat surface in a diamond shape (so the corner is facing you).
3. Place 1 slice cheese on wrapper.

Place about ¼ cup boudin sausage on the lower third of the wrapper. Top with about 1 tablespoon crumbled bacon. Fold the corner closest to you over the filling once, gently tucking it under the filling. Gently press down on each side of the filling to flatten the wrapper. Fold over both the left and right sides of the wrapper toward the middle. Brush the egg yolk over the opposite corner of the egg roll wrapper, taking care only to brush the wrapper itself. With your finger on the top of the roll, continue tightly rolling into a tube shape until completely sealed. Set aside. Repeat with remaining wrappers and fillings.
4. In a small bowl, stir together mustard and Zippy-Zap Sauce.
5. Working in batches, fry, turning occasionally, until golden brown, about 3 to 4 minutes. Remove with a slotted spoon, and let drain on prepared pan. Serve immediately with mustard sauce.

 **HOT TIP:** You can buy boudin at most grocery stores in the South. If you can't find it, lots of butchers in Louisiana and Texas will ship some to you anywhere in the country.

Cow Pie

Makes 8 to 10 servings

Now this ain't the kind of cow pie you might be thinking of at first. This kind here has layers of beef, potatoes, chiles, and cheeses. It's just what you're gonna want after a long day on the farm.

2 pounds ground beef
3 cloves garlic, minced
1 medium white onion, chopped
1 fresh jalapeño, chopped
1 (10-ounce) can diced tomatoes with green chiles
1 (1-ounce) package chili seasoning*
½ cup water
1 large russet potato (about ¾ pound), cut into ¼-inch-thick slices
1 (8-ounce) block Monterey Jack cheese with peppers, shredded
½ teaspoon cayenne pepper
½ teaspoon ground black pepper
1 (4-ounce) can chopped mild green chiles (undrained)
1½ cups sour cream
1 (8-ounce) block Cheddar cheese, shredded

1. Preheat oven to 350°. Lightly grease a 13x9-inch baking dish with cooking spray.
2. In a large nonstick skillet, cook and crumble ground beef over medium-high heat, stirring frequently, until browned, 8 to 10 minutes. Add garlic, onion, and jalapeño; cook, stirring frequently, until vegetables are tender, 4 to 5 minutes. Add tomatoes, chili seasoning, and ½ cup water. Reduce heat to low, cover, and let simmer, stirring occasionally, until ready to use.
3. In a medium saucepan, add potato slices and water to cover; bring to a boil over medium-high heat. Reduce heat, and let simmer until potato slices are partially cooked, 6 to 8 minutes. Drain and pat dry with paper towels.
4. In prepared dish, layer meat mixture, potato slices, and Monterey Jack cheese; sprinkle evenly with cayenne pepper and black pepper.
5. In a small bowl, mix together chiles and sour cream. Spread evenly over potato mixture. Sprinkle with Cheddar cheese.
6. Bake until bubbly and cheese is melted, 25 to 30 minutes. Let stand 10 minutes. Serve warm.

*I use Williams Chili Seasoning Mix.

Fried Red Tacos

Makes 15 tacos

The pork in this recipe is fall-apart tender after cooking for 4 hours. Then, you use the flavor-packed cooking liquid to dip the tortillas in and turn them red. If you've never had a red taco, you better try this one.

5   pounds boneless pork shoulder, cut into 2-inch pieces
5   cloves garlic
2   fresh jalapeños, quartered
2   medium carrots, cut into 1-inch pieces
1   medium white onion, cut into 8 wedges
1½   ounces dried guajillo peppers, stemmed and seeded
2   large tomato bouillon cubes
1   (6-ounce) can tomato paste
1½   teaspoons kosher salt
1½   teaspoons chili powder
¾   teaspoon ground black pepper
½   teaspoon ground cumin
½   small white onion, chopped
½   cup roughly chopped fresh cilantro
2   tablespoons fresh lime juice
15   fajita-size flour tortillas
2   (8-ounce) packages shredded Colby-Jack cheese blend

1. In a large Dutch oven, add pork, garlic, jalapeños, carrots, onion wedges, dried peppers, bouillon, tomato paste, salt, chili powder, black pepper, cumin, and water to cover by ½ inch. Cover and cook over medium-low heat until meat is tender, about 4 hours. Remove meat, and set aside. Drain vegetables, reserving broth (about 5 cups).

2. In the container of a blender, add vegetables and 2 cups of reserved broth; process until smooth, 1 to 2 minutes.

3. In a large nonstick skillet, heat purée over medium-low heat until it starts to simmer, 3 to 5 minutes. Stir in chopped onion, cilantro, lime juice, and 1 cup reserved broth. Let simmer, stirring occasionally, until onion is tender, about 10 minutes. Meanwhile, shred meat, discarding fat.

4. Heat griddle to 350°.

5. Working in batches, dip 1 tortilla in remaining 2 cups reserved broth, and place on hot griddle. On half of tortilla, spoon ¼ cup shredded meat and 1½ tablespoons vegetable purée, and sprinkle with ¼ cup cheese. Fold tortilla over in half, and grill each side until browned and cheese is melted, 1 to 2 minutes per side. Continue with remaining tortillas, remaining meat, remaining vegetable purée, and remaining cheese. Serve warm.

Homemade Corn Dogs

Makes 4

When I was growing up, we didn't always have those fancy sticks in our corn dogs. Turns out, you don't need 'em. These Homemade Corn Dogs are better than what you can get at the state fair.

1   **(32-ounce) container chicken broth**
3   **tablespoons Pepper Belly Pete's Zippy-Zap Sauce, divided**
1   **tablespoon Worcestershire sauce**
1   **teaspoon onion powder**
1   **teaspoon garlic powder**
1   **teaspoon Cajun seasoning***
4   **bun-length hot dogs**
Vegetable oil, for frying
1   **cup all-purpose flour**
1   **cup yellow cornmeal**
2   **teaspoons baking powder**
1   **teaspoon kosher salt**
1¼   **cups whole buttermilk, room temperature**
1   **large egg**
2   **tablespoons unsalted butter, melted**
1   **tablespoon honey**
½   **cup yellow mustard**

1. In a 3-quart saucepan, heat broth over high heat. Add 1 tablespoon Zippy-Zap Sauce, Worcestershire, onion powder, garlic powder, and Cajun seasoning; let simmer for about 5 minutes. Add hot dogs; remove from heat, and let stand for 30 minutes. Remove and pat dry with paper towels. Set aside.

2. In a large Dutch oven, fill halfway with oil. Heat oil over medium-high heat until a deep-fry thermometer registers 375°. Line a baking sheet with paper towels.

3. In a medium bowl, whisk together flour, cornmeal, baking powder, and salt. Whisk in buttermilk, egg, butter, and honey until smooth.

4. In a small bowl, stir together mustard and remaining 2 tablespoons Zippy-Zap Sauce.

5. Pour batter in a tall glass until 1 inch from the top. Add 1 hot dog. Using your fingers, gently remove hot dog, making sure batter is stuck to hot dog. Fry, turning often, until golden brown, 3 to 4 minutes. Remove with tongs, and let drain on prepared pan. Repeat with remaining hot dogs and batter. Serve immediately with mustard sauce.

*I use Cajun Two-Step.

Mexican Fried Rice

Makes 6 to 8 servings

I love fried rice and decided to give it a try with some hot peppers, chili powder, and taco sauce—turns out, it's pretty good!

1½ cups ½-inch-sliced carrot
1½ pounds ground beef
1½ teaspoons garlic powder
1½ teaspoons onion powder
1½ teaspoons chili powder
1½ teaspoons ground black pepper
½ teaspoon ground cumin
½ teaspoon dried Mexican oregano
2 cups chopped white onion
2 cups pepper strips (use a mix of bell pepper, fresh jalapeño, and serrano peppers)
¼ cup unsalted butter
2 cups cooked and chilled long-grain rice
1 tablespoon granulated tomato bouillon with chicken flavor
½ cup taco sauce, divided
1 cup fresh corn kernels
Pepper Belly Pete,s Zippy-Zap Sauce, to taste

1. In a small saucepan, combine carrot and water to cover. Bring to a boil over high heat. Cook until mostly tender, about 4 minutes. Drain.

2. In a large bowl, add beef, garlic powder, onion powder, chili powder, black pepper, cumin, and oregano. Mix with hands until well combined.

3. Heat a 12-inch cast-iron skillet over medium-high heat. Add beef mixture, and cook and crumble until browned, 10 to 12 minutes. Add carrot, onion, and pepper strips; cook until vegetables are softened, about 5 minutes, stirring frequently. Remove beef mixture from skillet.

4. Add butter to skillet. When butter melts, add rice, bouillon, and ¼ cup taco sauce, stirring to combine. Fold in beef mixture, corn, and remaining ¼ cup taco sauce. Stir in Zippy-Zap Sauce to taste. Serve hot.

HOT TIP: If you've got a big outside griddle, you can make this recipe outdoors. If you have trouble finding taco sauce where you are, you can use tomato sauce instead.

Texas Macaroni and Cheese

Makes about 16 servings

This is a great one-pot dinner—you've got vegetables, meat, and pasta that can all cook in the same Dutch oven. Not to mention, it's got Texas-shaped pasta, and anything with Texas is always better.

1	pound bacon, chopped
3	pounds boneless skinless chicken thighs, cubed
4	tablespoons Cajun seasoning*, divided
1½	teaspoons ground black pepper
3	cups chopped white onion
2	cups chopped red bell pepper
2	cups chopped celery
2	tablespoons Worcestershire sauce
2	tablespoons Pepper Belly Pete's Zippy-Zap Sauce
2	tablespoons minced garlic
1	(10.5-ounce) can cream of chicken soup
1	(10.5-ounce) can cream of mushroom soup
1	(16-ounce) block pasteurized processed cheese product*, cubed
1	(10.5-ounce) can tomatoes with green chiles
16	ounces Texas-shaped macaroni*
1	(32-ounce) container chicken broth

1. In a large Dutch oven, cook bacon over medium-high heat until crispy, 8 to 10 minutes. Remove with a slotted spoon, reserving drippings in the pot. Let drain on paper towels.

2. While bacon is cooking, season chicken with 2 tablespoons Cajun seasoning and black pepper. Add chicken to Dutch oven with bacon grease. Cook chicken until cooked through, about 10 minutes, stirring occasionally. Remove chicken from pot with a slotted spoon, reserving drippings in the pot.

3. In the same Dutch oven, add onion, bell pepper, celery, Worcestershire, and Zippy-Zap Sauce; cook, stirring occasionally, until vegetables are soft, about 10 minutes. Add minced garlic, soups, cheese, tomatoes, and remaining 2 tablespoons Cajun seasoning, stirring to combine. Add bacon, chicken, macaroni, and chicken broth, stirring well; bring to a gentle boil. Reduce heat to medium, and let simmer, covered, until macaroni is tender, 20 to 25 minutes. Let stand about 5 minutes before serving.

I use Cajun Two-Step, Velveeta cheese, and Skinner Texaroni Macaroni.

CHAPTER 8

OUTDOOR COOKING

THERE AIN'T MUCH BETTER THAN GRILLING, SMOKING, FRYING, AND BOILING OUTSIDE. YOU GET TO BE IN NATURE AND COOK UP SOMETHING GOOD! THESE ARE SOME OF MY FAVORITE OUTDOOR RECIPES.

Turkey Smash Burger

Makes 10

I cook these outside on my Blackstone, but you can use an indoor griddle, if you like. Change up the toppings to whatever suits you best—there ain't a wrong way to do it.

2   pounds ground turkey (85/15)
3   cloves garlic, minced
1   small white onion, grated
1   fresh jalapeño, grated
1½   teaspoons Cajun seasoning*
1½   teaspoons smoked paprika
1½   teaspoons ground black pepper
2   large eggs, lightly beaten
2   tablespoons Pepper Belly Pete's Flavor-Time Sizzling Steak Sauce
10   slices Monterey Jack cheese with peppers
1   large white onion, sliced
Stone-ground mustard, to taste
10   hamburger buns
2   large tomatoes, sliced and divided
4   cups baby spinach leaves, divided
Pepper Belly Pete's Zippy-Zap Sauce, to serve

1. In a large bowl, combine turkey, garlic, grated onion, jalapeño, Cajun seasoning, paprika, black pepper, eggs, and Sizzling Steak Sauce, using your hands to mix well. Shape into 10 equal balls.

2. Heat griddle to medium-high heat. Place balls on hot griddle. Place a foil-wrapped skillet or a spatula over the turkey balls, and smash them into flat disks. Smash each burger for 10 seconds, one at a time, applying a lot of pressure. Repeat until all the burgers are smashed.

3. Cook until internal temperature reaches 165°, 2 to 3 minutes per side. Place 1 slice cheese on each burger during the last minute of cooking.

4. Place onion slices on griddle, and cook until softened and browned, about 3 to 4 minutes per side.

5. Spread mustard on cut side of each bun. Place 1 patty on bottom half of each bun. Divide grilled onion, tomato slices, and spinach evenly among burgers. Top each burger with top half of bun. Serve with Zippy-Zap Sauce, if desired.

I use Cajun Two-Step.

Rib Eye Steaks

Makes 4

**This is a good, solid rib eye recipe. Sometimes, you don't need to overdo it.
This one hits just right.**

1½ **tablespoons beef and chop seasoning***
3 **teaspoons kosher salt, divided**
2 **teaspoons garlic powder**
2 **teaspoons onion powder**
2 **teaspoons ground black pepper**
4 **rib eye steaks**
Olive oil, for brushing
2 **medium yellow onions, sliced about ½ inch thick**

1. Heat a grill to 500°, or heat a cast-iron grill pan over medium-high heat.
2. In a small bowl, mix together beef and chop seasoning, 2 teaspoons salt, garlic powder, onion powder, and pepper.
3. Brush steaks with oil, and rub with seasoning mix.
4. Place steaks on grill or grill pan, and cook for 4 minutes per side for medium doneness. Remove from grill or grill pan.
5. Sprinkle onion slices with remaining 1 teaspoon salt. Cook onions on grill or grill pan until browned, about 3 to 4 minutes per side. Serve grilled onions with steak.

*I use Health Riles BBQ & Grilling Authentic Everyday Rub.

HOT TIP: I like to get my steaks from a local butcher when I can. I use 204 Meat Market because it's near my house and owned by my buddy Shane. Check out your local butcher shop to see what they have.

WATCH MY RECIPE VIDEO HERE.

Southern Fried Catfish

Makes 6 servings

Frying stuff inside can smell up your whole house—that's why I like to fry catfish outside on the patio. Wherever you want to cook it, it's sure to be a hit with your friends and family.

Vegetable oil, for frying
6	whole catfish, skinned and boned
½	cup yellow mustard
2	pounds yellow cornmeal
1	tablespoon ground black pepper
¾	tablespoon garlic powder
1½	teaspoons kosher salt
1½	teaspoons cayenne pepper

Pepper Belly Pete's Zippy-Zap Sauce, to serve

1. In a large skillet, fill halfway with oil. Heat oil over medium heat until a deep-fry thermometer registers 325°. Line a baking sheet with paper towels.

2. In a large bowl, toss fish with mustard until thoroughly coated.

3. In another large bowl, mix together cornmeal, black pepper, garlic powder, salt, and cayenne pepper.

4. Dredge each fish in cornmeal mixture, shaking off any extra.

5. Working in batches, fry fish until golden and flakes with a fork, 3 to 4 minutes, flipping halfway through. Remove with a slotted spoon, and let drain on prepared pan. Serve with Zippy-Zap Sauce, if desired.

Me and my dad when I was around 5 years old. We were fishing in Grandaddy Clyde's pond and caught some catfish.

Armadillo Tails

Makes 24

Some folks call these Texas Cabbage Rolls. No matter what you call 'em, they're gonna taste good.

1   **large head green cabbage (2½ pounds)**
12   **ounces smoked sausage, chopped**
1   **medium white onion, diced**
1   **fresh jalapeño, diced**
2   **teaspoons Cajun seasoning***
1   **teaspoon garlic powder**
1   **teaspoon ground black pepper**
1½   **cups diced green onion**
1   **(15-ounce) container ricotta cheese**
1   **tablespoon barbecue sauce**
1   **teaspoon Worcestershire sauce**
24   **slices bacon**

1. Wrap cabbage in plastic wrap, and freeze for 12 to 24 hours.
2. Remove head of frozen cabbage from the freezer, and set in cool water to thaw, about 1 hour.
3. In a medium nonstick skillet, cook smoked sausage over medium-high heat, stirring occasionally, until lightly browned, 3 to 4 minutes. Add onion, jalapeño, Cajun seasoning, garlic powder, and black pepper; cook, stirring frequently, until onions are soft, 3 to 4 minutes. Add green onion and ricotta, stirring until combined. Remove from heat, and stir in barbecue sauce and Worcestershire until well combined. Let filling cool slightly before using, about 20 minutes.
4. Cut bottom core away from cabbage. Remove leaves, and cut away hard part of the stems (about 24 leaves).
5. On a cutting board, lay 1 cabbage leaf flat, and place 1½ tablespoons filling on stem end. Roll up like a burrito, tucking ends of cabbage in while rolling. Take 1 slice bacon and tightly wrap around the full length of the cabbage roll, tucking the ends in. Repeat with remaining cabbage, remaining filling, and remaining bacon.
6. Heat a grill to 400° to 450°, or heat a cast-iron grill pan over medium-high heat. Working in batches, grill cabbage rolls, turning occasionally, until bacon is crisp, 4 to 5 minutes per side. Serve immediately.

*I use Cajun Two-Step.

HOT TIP: The reason I say to freeze and thaw your cabbage is because it makes it easier to peel the leaves off and roll them up into the Armadillo Tails.

Poor Man's Tacos

Makes 12

These are called **Poor Man's Tacos** because you can use a less expensive cut of meat and still get great taste. Use whatever you find on sale—no one will know you got a good deal on these because they taste like a million bucks.

1   teaspoon kosher salt
1   teaspoon garlic powder
1   teaspoon onion powder
1   teaspoon ground cumin
1   teaspoon dried Mexican oregano
1   teaspoon chili powder
1   teaspoon ground black pepper
1   pound thinly sliced boneless beef chuck shoulder steak or chuck eye steak
1   tablespoon olive oil
12   large fresh jalapeños
1   cup shredded Cheddar cheese, divided
12   street taco flour tortillas
Pepper Belly Pete's Zippy-Zap Sauce, to serve
Toppings: fresh chopped cilantro, chopped green onion

1. Heat a grill to 400° to 450°, or heat a cast-iron grill pan over medium-high heat.
2. In a small bowl, mix together salt, garlic powder, onion powder, cumin, oregano, chili powder, and black pepper.
3. Brush steak with oil, and rub with seasoning mix.
4. Cut down 1 side of each jalapeño. Using a spoon, carefully scoop out seeds and membrane, leaving stem attached.
5. Place steak on grill or grill pan, and cook in batches until charred, about 1½ to 2 minutes per side. (If using chuck eye steak, cook about 3 minutes per side.) Remove steak from grill or grill pan, and let rest for 5 minutes. Cut steak into thin strips, and chop.
6. Place jalapeños on grill or grill pan, cut side down, and cook for 2 to 3 minutes, turning to char all sides. Sprinkle ½ cup cheese evenly into jalapeño wells. Fill each with chopped steak, and sprinkle with remaining ½ cup cheese. Cook until cheese is melted, about 1 minute more. Remove from grill or grill pan.
7. Place tortillas on grill or grill pan, and cook until warmed, about 1 minute per side.
8. To serve, place jalapeño on a warmed tortilla. Serve with Zippy-Zap Sauce, if desired. Top with cilantro and green onion, if desired.

Shrimp Boil

Makes 10 to 12 servings

There's nothin' better than a neighborhood shrimp boil. I make this recipe using an outdoor boiler, but if you've got a pot big enough, you can make it on your stove.

10	quarts water
4	fresh lemons, quartered
3	fresh limes, quartered
2	pounds small red potatoes
1	pound smoked sausage, cut into 1-inch-thick rounds
10	sweet baby bell peppers
8	(4-inch) celery sticks
6	fresh jalapeños
3	small white onions, halved
1	head garlic, cut in half
1/3	cup minced garlic
2½	pounds shrimp boil seasoning mix
1	(5.2-ounce) container paprika
6	tablespoons lemon pepper
½	bottle Pepper Belly Pete's Zippy-Zap Sauce
3	pounds deveined easy-peel large fresh shrimp, unpeeled
2	(6-count) bags frozen mini corn on the cob
1	(8-ounce) package fresh whole button mushrooms

Fresh lemon wedges and Pepper Belly Pete's Zippy-Zap Sauce, to serve

1. In a 24-quart stockpot, add 10 quarts water, and bring to a boil over high heat; add lemons, limes, and potatoes, and cook for about 10 minutes.

2. Add sausage, bell peppers, celery, jalapeños, onions, garlic head, minced garlic, shrimp boil seasoning, paprika, lemon pepper, and Zippy-Zap Sauce; bring mixture to a rolling boil over high heat. Add shrimp. Remove from heat, and add corn and mushrooms. Cover and let stand until shrimp are pink and firm, 20 minutes.

3. Drain and serve with fresh lemon wedges and Zippy-Zap Sauce.

Sweet and Spicy Buffalo Ribs

Makes 4 to 6 servings

These juicy ribs are finger-lickin' good. If you're having a lot of people over, you might need to double the recipe. Folks are gonna want to take any leftovers to go.

1   slab St. Louis ribs (2½ to 3 pounds)
1   (16-ounce) bottle zesty Italian dressing
2   teaspoons kosher salt
2   teaspoons garlic powder
2   teaspoons onion powder
2   teaspoons smoked paprika
2   teaspoons ground black pepper
½   cup unsalted butter
½   cup granulated sugar
½   cup Pepper Belly Pete's Zippy-Zap Sauce
Pepper Belly Pete's Bacon Bourbon Barbecue Sauce, to serve

1. Using a sharp knife, pierce thin membrane on back of ribs, and peel to remove; discard.

2. Place ribs, bone side down, in a disposable foil pan. Pour Italian dressing over ribs. Turn ribs over so bone side is up, making sure to coat ribs with dressing. Cover and refrigerate for at least 4 hours or overnight.

3. Remove ribs from dressing, discarding dressing, and pat dry with paper towels. Sprinkle ribs evenly with salt, garlic powder, onion powder, paprika, and pepper. Press seasoning into ribs (do not rub). Let stand for 20 to 30 minutes.

4. Spray a grill rack with cooking spray. Preheat one side of grill to low heat (250° to 300°). Place ribs on opposite side of grill, bone side down. Grill, covered, over indirect heat for 3 hours.

5. In a medium saucepan, melt butter, sugar, and Zippy-Zap Sauce over medium heat until sugar is dissolved, stirring occasionally.

6. Place ribs in a clean large disposable foil pan. Pour butter mixture evenly over ribs. Cover tightly with foil. Grill over indirect heat until internal temperature registers 207°, about 20 minutes more. Remove ribs from grill. Serve warm with Bourbon Bacon Barbecue Sauce.

STEP-BY-STEP

If you've never grilled ribs before, it's time to give it a try. It's a great recipe to make when you've got folks coming over to watch the game or hang out for a summer barbecue. It's just good party food, if you ask me!

1. Remove the membrane from the back of the ribs. I sometimes use my teeth for this. You can also use a knife to cut it and your hands to pull it off.

2. Marinate the ribs with Italian dressing and let them sit in the fridge overnight.

3. The next day, season the ribs and press in the seasoning.

4. Grill them up over indirect heat for about 3 hours.

5. Pull them off the grill and pour the sauce from step 5 on page 204 on them. Wrap them up and put them back on the grill for just a little longer.

6. Serve them up with my Bacon Bourbon Barbecue Sauce.

There ain't much I like better than sitting out back with a cold beer in my hand while my dinner cooks. If you're not a regular griller, I suggest you get out there and try it with some of the recipes in this chapter. Whether you like cooking up steaks, wild game, or vegetables, I think using a grill is always a good call. You just can't beat the smoky, charged flavor that comes from grilling.

DON'T OVERTHINK IT

There are good things about charcoal grills, gas grills, and cast-iron grill pans. Use what you have. It might take some practice to figure out all the particulars of your grilling equipment, but it's worth it. Once you get the hang of it, you'll be grilling everything in sight.

SPICE IT UP

Season your food well, probably more than you think is necessary, before cooking. If you're using rubs with a lot of sugar, you want to cook over indirect heat so it doesn't burn. And sauces should come at the end after you've removed food from the grill.

TEMPERATURE MATTERS

Let your meat sit out for 30 minutes before grilling. You don't want to put cold meat on the grill. Then make sure to cover your grill while food is cooking to circulate heat.

BE PREPARED

Don't just put your food on and walk away. You need to watch for flare-ups. If it gets too hot, move your food to the other side of the grill. Keep long tongs handy in case you gotta make a quick grab.

Hot Water Cornbread

Makes 14 servings

I don't see many folks making Hot Water Cornbread these days, but most people's grandparents will remember it. This can be served with just about anything, and it's good every time. I usually fry this one outside on my patio, but it works just as well inside.

Peanut oil, for frying
2   cups yellow cornmeal
½   cup all-purpose flour
1   tablespoon cayenne pepper
1   teaspoon kosher salt
1   teaspoon ground black pepper
4   cups water
Pepper Belly Pete's Zippy-Zap Sauce,
       to serve

1. In a large cast-iron skillet, fill halfway with oil. Heat oil over medium-high heat until a deep-fry thermometer registers 350°. Line a baking sheet with paper towels.
2. In a large bowl, mix together cornmeal, flour, cayenne pepper, salt, and black pepper. Make a well in center.
3. In a medium saucepan, bring 4 cups water to a boil. Slowly add boiling water in center of cornmeal, stirring constantly. You want it thick, not mushy. (You may not use all the water.)
4. Spoon cornmeal mixture by heaping tablespoonfuls into hot oil, and fry, turning once, until it's as browned as you like it, about 2 to 3 minutes per side. Remove with a slotted spoon, and let drain on prepared pan. Serve with Zippy-Zap Sauce, if desired.

CHAPTER 9

SATISFYING SIDES

JUST BECAUSE SOMETHING IS A SIDE DISH
DOESN'T MEAN IT HAS TO PLAY SECOND
FIDDLE. THESE RECIPES ARE ALL GREAT
IN THEIR OWN RIGHT. IT'S GONNA BE
HARD TO PICK A FAVORITE.

Extreme Broccoli and Cheese Casserole

Makes 8 to 10 servings

This recipe will have folks who don't even like broccoli asking for seconds. They better like cheese, though, because I packed as much as I could in this one.

½ cup unsalted butter
1 (2-pound) head cauliflower, cut into florets
1 large white onion, chopped
1½ teaspoons garlic powder
1½ teaspoons cayenne pepper
1½ teaspoons smoked paprika
1½ teaspoons ground black pepper
1 (10.5-ounce) can cream of chicken soup
1½ cups half-and-half
2 tablespoons Pepper Belly Pete's Zippy-Zap Sauce, plus more to serve
1 tablespoon Worcestershire sauce
4 cups shredded American cheese
1 (8-ounce) package cream cheese, softened
4 cups shredded cooked white meat chicken
6 cups broccoli florets
2 cups shredded mozzarella cheese, divided
2 cups shredded Cheddar cheese, divided

1. Preheat oven to 350°. Lightly grease a 13x9-inch baking dish with cooking spray.
2. In a large Dutch oven, melt butter over medium-high heat. Add cauliflower, onion, garlic powder, cayenne pepper, paprika, black pepper, soup, half-and-half, Zippy-Zap Sauce, Worcestershire, American cheese, and cream cheese. Cook, stirring constantly, until cheeses are melted. Add chicken and broccoli. Reduce heat to low, and cook, stirring occasionally, until cauliflower and broccoli begin to soften, about 10 minutes.
3. Spoon half of broccoli mixture into prepared dish, and top with 1 cup mozzarella and 1 cup Cheddar. Spoon remaining broccoli mixture on top of cheese, and top with remaining 1 cup mozzarella and remaining 1 cup Cheddar. Cover with foil.
4. Bake, covered, for 45 minutes. Uncover and bake until bubbly, about 15 minutes more. Serve with Zippy-Zap Sauce, if desired.

Deep-Fried Deviled Eggs

Makes 12 eggs

Maybe you've heard of those fancy Scotch eggs? This is the country version of that idea. I don't know why you'd even serve an egg if it's not deviled.

Vegetable oil, for frying
6   large hard-boiled eggs, halved lengthwise
2   tablespoons mayonnaise
2   teaspoons dill pickle relish
1   teaspoon yellow mustard
⅛   teaspoon kosher salt
⅛   teaspoon ground black pepper
⅓   cup all-purpose flour
⅓   cup cornstarch
2   large eggs, lightly beaten
⅔   cup seasoned bread crumbs
Cajun seasoning*, to taste

1. In a medium Dutch oven, fill halfway with oil. Heat over medium-high heat until a deep-fry thermometer registers 350°. Line a baking sheet with paper towels.
2. Remove firm egg yolks from hard-boiled egg whites.
3. In a medium bowl, mash egg yolks. Add mayonnaise, relish, mustard, salt, and pepper, stirring to combine. Cover and refrigerate until ready to use.
4. Fill a small bowl with water.
5. In a second small bowl, combine flour and cornstarch.
6. In a third small bowl, place beaten eggs.
7. In a fourth small bowl, add bread crumbs.
8. Dip each hard-boiled egg white in water, then flour mixture, then beaten eggs, then bread crumbs.
9. Working in batches, drop breaded egg whites into hot oil, and fry until golden, 2 to 3 minutes. Drain on prepared baking sheet. Let cool slightly. Fill with egg yolk mixture. Sprinkle with Cajun seasoning to taste. Serve immediately.

*I use Cajun Two-Step.

Charro Beans

Makes 10 cups

**If you like things spicy, this dish is for you. You can take it down a notch
if needed. Be warned: this one brings the heat.**

2   **smoked ham hocks**
1   **pound dried pinto beans,
     washed and sorted**
5   **cloves garlic, chopped**
2   **fresh jalapeños, chopped**
2   **cups chopped plum tomatoes**
1   **large white onion, chopped**
2   **tablespoons tomato bouillon
     with chicken flavor***
1   **tablespoon ground cumin**
1   **tablespoon chili powder**
1   **tablespoon ground black
     pepper**
1   **cup Pepper Belly Pete's Extremely
     Hot Roasted Reaper Salsa**
Chili cheese pork rinds, to serve
**Toppings: fresh chopped cilantro,
     Pepper Belly Pete's Zippy-Zap
     Sauce**

1. In a large Dutch oven, add ham hocks,
beans, garlic, jalapeños, tomatoes, onion,
bouillon, cumin, chili powder, black pepper,
Roasted Reaper Salsa, and water to cover by
3 inches. Cover and cook over low heat until
beans are tender, about 3 hours.
2. Remove meat from ham hocks and chop;
discard bones (or reserve for another use).
Add meat back to Dutch oven with beans.
Serve over pork rinds, and top with cilantro
and Zippy-Zap Sauce, if desired.

**I use Knorr Caldo de Tomate con Sabor de
Pollo Tomato Bouillon with Chicken Flavor.*

My parents were
building a pond behind
the barn, and I climbed
up in the equipment to
pretend like I was doing
a little work myself.

Loaded Potato Soup Casserole

Makes 6 to 8 servings

Traditonal scalloped potatoes got a cowboy makeover with this recipe.
I've never met a casserole that wasn't made better by adding bacon—it's a
surefire win every time.

1	pound bacon, chopped
2	cups chopped white onion
1	tablespoon Pepper Belly Pete's Zippy-Zap Sauce
¼	cup unsalted butter
¼	cup all-purpose flour
1	tablespoon garlic powder
1	tablespoon onion powder
1	tablespoon ground black pepper
1	teaspoon cayenne pepper
1	(12-ounce) can plus ½ cup evaporated milk, divided
2	(8-ounce) blocks mild Cheddar cheese, shredded
2	pounds russet potatoes, peeled and cut into ¼-inch slices
1	(16-ounce) block smoked mozzarella cheese, shredded
½	cup chopped green onion (green parts only)

1. Preheat oven to 350°. Lightly grease a 13x9-inch baking dish with cooking spray.

2. In a 12-inch cast-iron skillet, cook bacon over medium heat until crispy, about 12 minutes. Remove with a slotted spoon, reserving drippings in the pan. Let drain on paper towels.

3. In the same skillet, cook onion and Zippy-Zap Sauce over medium-high heat until onions are tender, about 7 minutes. Add butter, flour, garlic powder, onion powder, black pepper, and cayenne pepper; stir until incorporated, 2 to 3 minutes. Add 12-ounce can evaporated milk, stirring to combine. Stir in remaining ½ cup evaporated milk, if needed, to thin mixture. Reduce heat to low, and stir in Cheddar cheese; cook until cheese is melted, 2 to 3 minutes. Remove from heat.

4. In prepared baking dish, layer half of the potatoes, overlapping as needed. Spoon cheese mixture over potatoes. Layer remaining potatoes over cheese mixture. Sprinkle with smoked mozzarella. Cover with foil.

5. Bake, covered, until potatoes are tender, about 1 hour and 10 minutes. Remove from oven, uncover, and sprinkle with cooked bacon and green onion. Bake until golden brown, 15 to 20 minutes more. Serve warm.

Spam Fries

Makes 4 servings

I know what you're thinking, but don't knock it 'til you try it. Spam gets a bad wrap, but it can be tasty when you fry it up.

Vegetable oil, for frying
1   (12-ounce) can pork luncheon meat*
2   large eggs
2   tablespoons water
2   cups panko (Japanese bread crumbs)
¼   cup cornstarch
Pepper Belly Pete's Zippy-Zap Sauce or ketchup, to serve

1. In a large cast-iron skillet, fill halfway with oil. Heat oil over medium-high heat until a deep-fry thermometer registers 375°. Line a baking sheet with paper towels.

2. Cut luncheon meat into 24 sticks.

3. In a medium bowl, whisk eggs and 2 tablespoons water until frothy.

4. In another medium bowl, combine bread crumbs and cornstarch.

5. Dip each stick in egg mixture, letting excess drip off. Roll in bread crumb mixture to cover.

6. Working in batches, fry sticks until crispy, 3 to 4 minutes, turning often. Remove with a slotted spoon, and let drain on prepared pan. Serve with Zippy-Zap Sauce or ketchup, if desired.

I use Spam.

Stuffed Alligator Pears

Makes 8

The only thing that makes alligator pears (or avocados, as some folks call them) better is stuffing them with chicken, seasonings, and jalapeño purée and then frying them up.

4 boneless skinless chicken thighs (about 1¼ pounds)
4 teaspoons Cajun seasoning*, divided
1 tablespoon vegetable oil, plus more for frying
1 (8-ounce) package shredded Monterey Jack cheese with peppers
2 tablespoons jalapeño pepper purée*
8 medium whole avocados, slightly soft
1 cup all-purpose flour
1½ cups whole buttermilk
1½ cups seasoned panko (Japanese bread crumbs)

1. Season chicken thighs with 2 teaspoons Cajun seasoning.
2. In a large cast-iron skillet, heat 1 tablespoon oil over medium-high heat; add chicken, and cook until a meat thermometer inserted in the thickest portion registers 165°, 3 to 4 minutes per side. Remove chicken from heat, and let cool slightly before dicing.
3. In a large Dutch oven, fill halfway with oil. Heat over medium-high heat until a deep-fry thermometer registers 350°. Line a baking sheet with paper towels.
4. In a medium bowl, stir together diced chicken, cheese, and jalapeño purée until combined.

5. Cut avocados in half and remove the seeds. Remove the skin and scoop out each avocado half, leaving about a ¼-inch border around the edge. Do not scoop all the way through the bottom or sides. Stir 1 cup scraped-out avocado into chicken mixture.
6. Pack the filling (about ½ cup) into each hollowed-out avocado half. Take the other half of the avocado and press together until it resembles a whole avocado again.
7. In a shallow dish, mix together flour and remaining 2 teaspoons Cajun seasoning.
8. In a medium bowl, add buttermilk.
9. In another medium bowl, add bread crumbs.
10. Roll avocado in flour mixture, then in buttermilk, and then in bread crumbs. Working in batches, fry avocados in hot oil until golden brown, about 3 minutes, turning occasionally. Let drain on prepared pan.

I use Cajun Two-Step and Louisiana Pepper Exchange Jalapeño Pepper Purée.

HOT TIP: Use avocados that are still mostly firm (too firm for good guacamole). They will hold up better when you scoop them out and fry them.

WATCH MY RECIPE VIDEO HERE.

Soup Beans

Makes 8 to 10 servings

Some things, like mashed potatoes and gravy, were just made to go together. That's how I feel about Soup Beans and Homemade Cornbread (page 227)—just can't have one without the other!

5	slices bacon, chopped
4	cloves garlic, chopped
2	large fresh jalapeños, chopped
1	large yellow onion, chopped
1	extra-large tomato bullion with chicken flavor cube
1	large smoked ham hock
2	pounds dried pinto beans, washed and sorted
1	tablespoon garlic powder
1	tablespoon Cajun seasoning*
1	tablespoon chili powder
1	tablespoon ground black pepper
½	teaspoon ground cumin
2	(32-ounce) containers chicken stock
8	cups water

Homemade Cornbread (recipe on page 227), to serve

1. In a 12-quart stockpot, cook bacon over medium-high heat until crispy, 6 to 8 minutes. Remove with a slotted spoon, reserving drippings in the pot. Let drain on paper towels.

2. In same pot, add garlic, jalapeños, onion, and bouillon; cook, stirring frequently, until onions are tender, 6 to 7 minutes. Add ham hock, beans, garlic powder, Cajun seasoning, chili powder, black pepper, cumin, chicken stock, and 8 cups water, stirring to combine. Cover and cook over medium-low heat, stirring every 45 minutes, until beans are tender, 2 hours and 30 minutes to 2 hours and 45 minutes. Remove ham hock before serving. Serve with Homemade Cornbread.

I use Cajun Two-Step.

Homemade Cornbread

Makes 4 to 6 servings

Everybody needs to have a good cornbread recipe in their back pocket
to get out when they hear company's coming. It makes a great side dish
for just about any recipe.

1	tablespoon vegetable shortening or lard
1½	cups self-rising yellow cornmeal
½	cup self-rising flour
½	teaspoon kosher salt
2	cups whole buttermilk
2	large eggs

1. Preheat oven to 425°.

2. In an 8-inch cast-iron skillet, place vegetable shortening, and bake until skillet is hot, about 5 minutes.

3. Meanwhile, in a medium bowl, whisk together cornmeal, flour, salt, buttermilk, and eggs. Pour into hot skillet.

4. Bake until a wooden pick inserted in center comes out clean, 18 to 20 minutes. Remove from oven. Serve warm.

Wylie and I love spending time together. This photo was taken during Halloween one year. He's got a great personality!

Vegetable Fritters

Makes about 10 servings

This is kinda like my Hot Water Cornbread recipe (page 209), but I like to add vegetables sometimes to give it a little kick. Some folks call these hush puppies. You can call them whatever you like, I'd just be sure to serve 'em with Zippy-Zap Sauce.

Vegetable oil, for frying
3   fresh jalapeños, diced
1   small white onion, diced
1   cup yellow corn kernels
1   teaspoon kosher salt
1   teaspoon ground black pepper
3   cups water
2   cups plain yellow cornmeal
½   cup all-purpose flour
1   tablespoon baking powder
Pepper Belly Pete's Zippy-Zap Sauce,
      to serve

1. In a large cast-iron skillet, fill halfway with oil. Heat oil over medium-high heat until a deep-fry thermometer registers 350°. Line a baking sheet with paper towels.
2. In a large saucepan, add jalapeños, onion, corn, salt, black pepper, and 3 cups water; bring to a boil over high heat. Reduce heat to medium, and let simmer for 10 minutes.
3. In a medium bowl, combine cornmeal, flour, and baking powder. Slowly add the hot vegetable water to cornmeal mixture, stirring constantly. You want it thick, not mushy. (You may not use all the water.)
4. Spoon cornmeal mixture by heaping tablespoons into hot oil, and fry, turning once, until it's as browned as you like it, about 2 to 3 minutes per side. Remove with a slotted spoon, and let drain on prepared pan. Serve with Zippy-Zap Sauce, if desired.

CHAPTER 10

DARN GOOD DESSERTS

REWARD YOURSELF FOR A HARD DAY'S
WORK WITH ONE OF THESE DESSERTS—
YOU'LL BE GLAD YOU DID.

Sour Cream Spice Pie

Makes 1 (9-inch) pie

This old pie recipe here has been around for a long time. It was my dad's absolute favorite, and it's one of my top three. Give it a try and see if you like it, too.

1½ **cups packed dark brown sugar**
½ **teaspoon ground allspice**
½ **teaspoon ground cinnamon**
¼ **teaspoon ground cloves**
⅛ **teaspoon kosher salt**
1½ **cups sour cream**
2 **large eggs**
1 **(9-inch) frozen deep-dish piecrust**
3 **large egg whites, room temperature**
6 **teaspoons granulated sugar**

1. Preheat oven to 425°.
2. In a large bowl, whisk together brown sugar, allspice, cinnamon, cloves, salt, sour cream, and eggs until well combined. Pour into piecrust.
3. Bake until crust has lightly browned, 10 minutes. Reduce oven temperature to 350°, and bake until set with a slight jiggle, 30 minutes more. Remove from oven.
4. Reduce oven temperatue to 300°.
5. In a medium bowl, beat egg whites with a hand mixer at high speed until foamy; slowly add granulated sugar, beating until stiff peaks form, about 5 minutes. Add topping to pie, and spread evenly on top, sealing to edges of crust.
6. Bake until topping is lightly browned, about 10 minutes. Let cool completely on a wire rack before serving.

I've always loved feeding Wylie. And he's always loved eating!

No-Bake Cowboy Cookies

Makes about 30

WATCH MY RECIPE
VIDEO HERE.

My son, who goes by Pepperoni Pete, loves making these cookies. This is a good recipe to get your kids cooking in the kitchen.

½ cup unsalted butter
1 (12-ounce) package semisweet chocolate chips
1 (10-ounce) package large marshmallows
1 cup sweetened condensed milk
4 cups frosted cornflakes cereal*
4 cups crisp rice cereal squares*
2 cups mini marshmallows

1. Line several baking sheets with wax paper.
2. In a large nonstick skillet, heat butter over low heat until melted, 2 to 3 minutes. Add chocolate chips, large marshmallows, and condensed milk. Cook, stirring constantly, until melted and combined. Add cereals and mini marshmallows, and mix together until combined. Remove from heat, and drop cookies by heaping tablespoonfuls onto prepared pans.
3. Place in refrigerator until the chocolate hardens and cookies can be easily removed from the wax paper, about 3 hours. Store in the refrigerator.

I use Kellogg's® Frosted Flakes® cereal and Rice Chex cereal.

Pepperoni Pete (Wylie) and I made a video doing our No-Bake Cowboy Cookies. We enjoy cooking together.

Strawberry Surprise

Makes 6 to 8 servings

**This recipe right here is great for potlucks and family get-togethers.
Kids young and old like this one, and it's hard to mess it up.**

1   **(14-ounce) prepared angel food cake, chopped**

1   **(14-ounce) can sweetened condensed milk**

1   **(14-ounce) bottle whole strawberry milk, shaken**

1   **(16-ounce) container frozen whipped topping, thawed**

2   **cups fresh strawberries, hulled and halved (about 16 strawberries)**

1. In a large bowl, stir together cake and condensed milk. Spoon into an 11x7-inch baking dish, and spread out evenly. Pour strawberry milk evenly over cake mixture. Top with whipped topping. Arrange cut strawberries on cake. Cover and refrigerate for at least 30 minutes before serving.

HOT TIP: You can make your own angel food cake or buy one premade at the grocery store.

My dad on a vacation with my mom in Niagara Falls in the 1990s.

Buttermilk Pie

Makes 1 (9-inch) pie

I love pie, and I think this is my all-time favorite one. It's also pretty easy to put together, so if you're new to making pies, this here is a good starter recipe.

1   **(9-inch) frozen deep-dish piecrust**
4   **large eggs**
¼   **cup unsalted butter, softened**
3   **tablespoons all-purpose flour**
1   **cup whole buttermilk**
1   **teaspoon vanilla extract**
¼   **teaspoon kosher salt**
2   **cups granulated sugar**

1. Preheat oven to 350°. Place frozen piecrust on a rimmed baking sheet.

2. In a medium bowl, beat eggs with a hand mixer at low speed just until lightly beaten. Add butter and flour, and beat until combined. Add buttermilk, vanilla extract, and salt, and beat until combined; slowly beat in sugar (some small bits of butter may remain). Pour into crust. (Do not overfill.)

3. Bake until set in the center, 45 minutes to 1 hour. Let cool completely on a wire rack before serving.

 **HOT TIP:** About 15 minutes into baking, you can add a foil ring around the crust to keep it from getting too brown.

Old-Fashioned Chocolate Fudge

Makes 24 pieces

Some people get nervous about trying to make homemade fudge.
It's not so hard if you follow these instructions. Your family will be glad
you gave it a try.

3   cups granulated sugar
²⁄₃   cup unsweetened cocoa powder
1½   cups whole milk
¼   cup unsalted butter, melted
1   teaspoon vanilla extract

1. Line an 11x7-inch baking dish with foil, letting ends of foil extend over edges of dish. Lightly grease foil with cooking spray.

2. Heat a large nonstick skillet over high heat; add sugar and cocoa powder, stirring to combine. Slowly add milk, and bring to a boil, stirring constantly to break up small clumps. Once at a boil, continue stirring for 1 to 2 minutes; reduce heat to medium, and cook until an instant-read thermometer registers 232°. Do not stir. Remove from heat.

3. Add in butter and vanilla extract. Do not stir. Let cool in pan until an instant-read thermometer registers 110°, about 35 minutes. Stir until well incorporated, and pour mixture into prepared pan. Let cool completely at room temperature before serving, about 4 hours. Lift from pan using foil as handles. Cut into squares.

 **HOT TIP:** Depending on the type of pan you use, it may take longer for the fudge mixture to reach or cool to certain temperatures.

Banana Pudding

Makes about 12 servings

This is an oldie but goody Southern recipe right here. You're gonna feel like you're back sitting in your meemaw's kitchen.

2½ cups granulated sugar

1 cup self-rising flour

2 (12-ounce) cans evaporated milk

6 tablespoons unsalted butter, melted

4 large egg yolks

2 teaspoons vanilla extract

3 cups sliced bananas, divided

3 cups vanilla wafer cookies, divided

1 (16-ounce) container frozen whipped topping, thawed

Toppings: whole and crushed vanilla wafer cookies

1. In a large bowl, whisk together sugar, flour, evaporated milk, butter, and egg yolks.

2. In a medium nonstick pot, add sugar mixture, and cook over low heat, stirring constantly, until thick and bubbly, about 15 minutes. Remove from heat, and stir in vanilla extract. Let cool for 30 minutes, stirring occasionally.

3. In a large serving bowl, add half of pudding mixture. Top with half of the sliced banana and then half of the cookies. Spread 2 cups whipped topping over cookies. Repeat layers once, spreading remaining whipped topping over the top. Top with whole and crushed cookies as desired. Cover and refrigerate for at least 1 hour before serving.

Chocolate Pie

Makes 1 (9-inch) pie

You ever met anyone who doesn't like chocolate pie? If so, I hope you're not friends with them anymore. It's just too good not to like.

1   (9-inch) frozen deep-dish piecrust
1½   cups plus 10 teaspoons granulated sugar, divided
6   tablespoons all-purpose flour
3   tablespoons unsweetened cocoa powder
1½   cups evaporated milk
3   tablespoons unsalted butter, softened
2   large egg yolks
1   teaspoon vanilla extract
5   large egg whites, room temperature

1. Bake piecrust according to package directions; let cool.

2. In a large bowl, whisk together 1½ cups sugar, flour, cocoa powder, evaporated milk, butter, and egg yolks until incorporated (some bits of butter will remain).

3. In a large stainless steel skillet, add filling mixture, and heat over medium-low heat, slowly whisking constantly, until butter starts to melt; stir in vanilla. Continue to cook until thickened and bubbly, about 12 minutes more. Mixture should hold its shape if you run a whisk through it. Immediately pour into prepared piecrust, and set aside while preparing topping.

4. Preheat oven to 300°.

5. In a medium bowl, beat egg whites with a hand mixer at high speed until foamy; slowly add remaining 10 teaspoons sugar, beating until stiff peaks form, 2 to 3 minutes.

6. Add topping to pie, and spread evenly on top, sealing to edges of crust. Place on a rimmed baking sheet.

7. Bake until topping is lightly browned, 10 to 13 minutes. Let cool completely on a wire rack before serving.

HOT TIP: With the chocolate filling, it's not about the time—it's about the consistency. You want to do it low and slow to get it to thicken up.

Fried Ice Cream

Makes 4 servings

If you haven't ever eaten fried ice cream, you're doing it wrong. This is quite possibly one of the best things on the planet.

4 (½-cup) scoops vanilla ice cream
Vegetable oil, for frying
3 **large egg whites**
2½ **cups crushed potato chips**
Toppings: powdered sugar, chocolate syrup

1. Place each ice cream scoop in the center of an 8-inch piece of plastic wrap. Wrap tightly in a ball, and freeze for at least 6 hours or overnight.
2. In a large countertop fryer, fill halfway with oil. Heat oil over medium-high heat until a deep-fry thermometer registers 375°. Line a baking sheet with paper towels.
3. Whisk egg whites in a medium bowl until frothy, almost to soft peak.
4. In another medium bowl, place potato chips.
5. Working with one scoop at a time, unwrap ice cream ball. Dip in egg whites, tossing to coat. Toss in potato chips. Place in a fryer basket.
6. Fry, one at a time, until lightly golden brown, about 20 seconds; repeat with remaining balls. Top each ball with powdered sugar and chocolate syrup, if desired. Serve immediately.

Bowl of Gold

Makes 8 to 10 servings

If you take this dessert to a gathering, you're coming back with an empty bowl every time. Guaranteed.

1   **(8-ounce) block cream cheese, softened**
2   **(3.4-ounce) packages instant vanilla pudding mix**
4   **cups whole milk**
1   **teaspoon vanilla extract**
3   **cups crushed vanilla sandwich cookies***

1. In a medium bowl, beat cream cheese with a hand mixer at high speed until fluffy. Add pudding mix to the bowl, then slowly add milk while beating on medium speed until cream cheese is incorporated and pudding is thick, 2 to 3 minutes. Beat in vanilla extract.

2. In a large serving bowl, place 1 cup crushed cookies on the bottom; layer half the pudding on top of cookies. Top with 1 cup crushed cookies. Layer remaining half of pudding, and top with remaining 1 cup crushed cookies. Cover and refrigerate at least 1 hour before serving.

*I use Golden Oreos, but you can substitute any vanilla sandwich cookie, like Keebler Vienna Fingers Vanilla Fudge Crème.

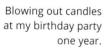

Blowing out candles at my birthday party one year.

Tiger Fudge

Makes about 12 servings

This fudge has peanut butter and chocolate in it—it don't get much better than that. Be careful of entering this one in your next county fair. You'll be coming home with all the blue ribbons after those judges get one taste of this.

½   cup plus 2 tablespoons unsalted butter, divided
3   cups granulated sugar
⅔   cup evaporated milk
1   teaspoon marshmallow crème*
1½ cups creamy peanut butter
2   teaspoons vanilla extract, divided
6   ounces semisweet chocolate chips
½   cup sweetened condensed milk

1. Line an 11x7-inch baking dish with foil, letting ends of foil extend over edges of dish. Lightly grease foil with cooking spray.

2. In a large nonstick skillet, melt ½ cup butter over medium heat; stir in sugar and evaporated milk. Bring to a low boil, and cook, stirring constantly, for 5 minutes. Remove from heat; stir in marshmallow crème, peanut butter, and 1 teaspoon vanilla extract until smooth. Remove from heat. Leave in pan (this will keep mixture warm).

3. In a medium microwave-safe bowl, add chocolate chips, condensed milk, and remaining 2 tablespoons butter. Microwave on medium until melted and smooth, about 2 minutes, stirring every 30 seconds. Add remaining 1 teaspoon vanilla extract, and stir until smooth.

4. Pour peanut butter mixture into prepared pan. Dollop chocolate mixture by tablespoonfuls on top of peanut butter mixture. Using the tip of a sharp knife, swirl chocolate into peanut butter mixture, working quickly before it cools. Refrigerate until firm, about 6 hours. Lift from pan using foil as handles. Cut into squares.

I use Kraft Jet-Puffed Marshmallow Crème.

RECIPE INDEX

EDITORIAL

Founder
Phyllis Hoffman DePiano

President/Chief Creative Officer
Brian Hart Hoffman

EVP/Chief Content Officer
Brooke Michael Bell

Editorial Director Anna Hartzog

Art Director Karissa Brown

Project Editor Kristi Fleetwood

Assistant Project Editor Savannah Donald

Senior Copy Editor Meg Lundberg

Copy Editor Kellie Keeling

Test Kitchen Director Laura Crandall

Food Stylists
Aaron Conrad, Katie Dickerson,
Kathleen Kanen, and Vanessa Rocchio

Prop Stylists Lucy Finney, Maggie Hill

Photographers
Jim Bathie and Kyle Carpenter

Senior Digital Imaging Specialist
Delisa McDaniel

PRODUCTION & MARKETING

President/Chief Executive Officer
Eric Hoffman

EVP/Chief Operating Officer
Greg Baugh

EVP/Chief Marketing Officer
Missy Polhemus

VP/Marketing Kristy Harrison

Marketing Coordinator
Morgan Barbay

THANK Y'ALL

I'VE GOT LOTS OF FOLKS TO THANK
who helped make this cookbook happen.
First, I want to thank my wife, Sara, and son,
Wylie. They have both been very supportive as
things have taken off with this whole Pepper
Belly Pete adventure. I'd also like to thank my
friends and family who have been encouraging
and came over to celebrate the cookbook
launch with me last summer: Jack, Pete, Shane,
Kyle, Julie, Brooklee, and Tim. Thank you to the
team at Hoffman Media who traveled to Texas
and spent time working on my cookbook:
Anna, Kathleen, Maggie, and Kyle. A big thank
you to my social media followers and viewers
for trying my recipes and coming back for
more. This has been a wild ride, and I can't
wait to see what happens next.